D1557293

PARTRIDGES

Their Breeding and Management

PARTRIDGES

Their Breeding and Management

G. E. S. Robbins

The Boydell Press

© G.E.S. Robbins 1984

First published 1984
for the World Pheasant Association
by the Boydell Press
an imprint of Boydell & Brewer Ltd
PO Box 9 Woodbridge Suffolk IP12 3DF

ISBN 0 85115 191 4

Printed in Great Britain by Bulls Frieson Limited
Malvern House, Littlers Close,
Merton, SW19

CONTENTS

ACKNOWLEDGEMENTS

The World Pheasant Association kindly agreed to publish this book for which I am most grateful, and wish them every success for the future. Also I would like to express my appreciation to Iain Grahame, Keith Howman, and Keith Chalmers-Watson for their guidance and encouragement. My thanks to Dr Dick Potts, and Dr John Beer, of the Game Conservancy for their help and advice. Finally, to Wendy, Johanna and Sarah our daughters, who endured a lot during the writing of this book.

G.E.S. Robbins

FOREWORD

I suppose that at least 90% of the world literature on partridges deals with only three species and nearly all of that literature, well over 1,350 works, concerns only one species; *Perdix perdix.*

The remaining species, about 44 of them, are virtually unknown, yet just as interesting and in many cases just as vulnerable to changes in their environment. The tropical and woodland species are particularly difficult to study in the field and I am sure that aviculture has a most important role to play in helping us to understand their behavioural ecology and thus in aiding their conservation in the wild.

Most aviculturists have not been much attracted to the partridge and perhaps they are not as splendid as most of the pheasants. Whatever the reason the methods of maintaining partridges in aviaries is largely unknown. This book will thus fill many important gaps in our knowledge of partridge aviculture and encourage others to complete the picture.

Dr G.R. Potts
Director of Research
The Game Conservancy,
Fordingbridge, Hants SP6 1 EF

CHAPTER 1

INTRODUCTION

After taking on the challenge to write my first book on Quail*
and after its excellent reception worldwide from beginners and
experienced aviculturists alike, I was persuaded to write a similar
book on Partridge. However, I decided that to cover the whole
family, which includes Francolin, was too much of a task with the
limited time available for research.

This volume is confined to the 47 species of Partridge while a
similar number of Francolin will be covered in a further book
devoted to themselves. This book is not intended as a monograph on
the Partridge of the world, but rather as a basic handbook for those
interested in their breeding and management. Partridge found
around the world can be split into two types: tropical and non-
tropical. The non-tropical species in general can be further split into
those kept for sporting purposes and those rarer species kept by the
aviculturist for pleasure and as a breeding pool for long term
conservation. The main part of this book is devoted to the general
management and breeding of species raised for non-sporting
purposes. There are many books already available on birds for
sporting purposes, therefore this must be regarded as a basic guide
for the beginner when starting with Partridges for the first time, and
may give those who are a little more experienced a few useful tips on
new species they might wish to keep.

As with all sectors of aviculture, methods and techniques are
constantly being challenged and changed. Some of the items
mentioned in this book may become out of date in time, or not be
suitable for your particular climate or situation. Hopefully you will
find this book of help to you in the future, to enjoy the challenge of
breeding these fascinating birds.

G.E.S. Robbins
Mendlesham, Suffolk, 1983

Quail. Their Breeding and Management
World Pheasant Association. 1981

CHAPTER 2

AVIARIES

Aviary Selection

There are many types of housing used by the aviculturist to keep his birds, and his choice is dictated by three factors: space, finance, and existing facilities. In addition, there are the personal likes and dislikes of the individual as to whether he thinks his birds should be kept on wire, sand, or a soil floor, and to what extent tropical species need to be protected from the elements. I propose to develop each of these points to help the beginner to make his decision regarding the type of accommodation required.

Space Requirement

Partridge provide the aviculturist with another unique opporunity of keeping members of the Galliformes family without having to provide a large amount of space such as is required by pheasants, grouse and guans. The person who only has a small garden or backyard can easily accommodate six of the smaller species within an area of 36' x 6' (11m x 1.8m), whereas the pheasant breeder might only be able to house one pair of small Peacock Pheasants in such an area. Therefore, having only a small plot available does not stop the keeping of these interesting birds. One word of warning — certain species do have a penetrating call, particularly during the breeding season, which might upset neighbours if they are housed too close.

Finance

While it remains for each individual to decide how much he is willing to spend, the size of pens falls within the scope of a handyman using new or second hand materials. The various types of housing will be discussed in more detail later in the chapter.

Existing Facilities

Partridge often appeal to the person who already keeps other birds, and are small enough to accommodate the bottom of an aviary. One prime rule must be remembered — that adult pairs of

Partridge must not be housed together, or with any other of the Galliformes, as they will fight, especially during the breeding season. Housing with other birds, such as finches or softbills can be very successful and utilises the floor space available. There are two major dislikes of the less hardy species of Partridge, damp and draughts, which must be borne in mind when housing in an existing aviary. Suitable cover and a day area must be available at all times. There is a further consideration to be taken into account; certain species do perch, and will fly up to roost, thus disturbing the other occupants.

Accommodation

For the serious breeder of Partridge, pairs should be housed on their own, so that their breeding performance can be recorded, eggs identified, ailments kept to the minimum. The best possible accommodation should be provided for obvious reasons; an old structure of rusty wire on a second hand frame does not enhance the appearance of the occupants or provide the best environment for the birds to be kept in good health and allow them to breed. There is also the need to undertake running repairs at regular intervals, which if not carried out, could result in a valuable bird being lost. In general, the aviculturist will agree that money spent on a good design and long-life materials are well worth the extra investment.

Size

There are a number of schools of thought as to the space required to house various species of Partridge, and aviculturists seem to have differing views in various parts of the world. In America, Partridge are often kept in small wire cages housed in a shed for the winter period, and then transferred to an outside house consisting of a wire run raised off the ground and having a weatherproof enclosure at one end, with a total area of some 6' x 2' (1.8m x 0.6m); others house their stock in larger units 8' x 3' (2.5m x 0.9m). My own preference is for an aviary on the ground of approximately 6' x 6' (1.8m x 1.8m), to accommodate one medium size breeding pair, ensuring they are maintained in good condition. A good covering of sharp sand to a depth of at least 2" (5cm) is preferable to using wire floors; this requirement has been developed over a number of years and has proved to be very satisfactory.

Materials
Suitable housing can be constructed from a variety of materials, timber, wire, galvanised, asbestos, and polythene sheet

Netting
Sparrows and various other vermin must be prevented from entering your aviaries, therefore the choice of the correct size of netting is most important. Should the breeder decide to allow his stock to raise their own chicks, the wire size required must be very small, certainly less than ¾" mesh (1.9cm); for general use and around the base of the aviary ½" mesh (1.3cm) will satisfy most requirements; always remember that if your aviary does not have a wire bottom and is placed on the ground, the sides should have wire mesh fixed and extended out around the edges of the aviary for at least 12" (30.5cm) to prevent vermin digging under the walls.

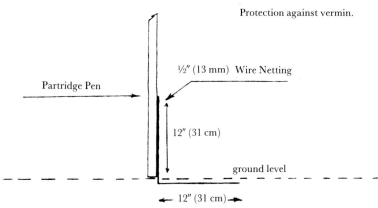

Protection against vermin.

Partridge Pen

½" (13 mm) Wire Netting

12" (31 cm)

ground level

◄— 12" (31 cm) —►

To prevent sparrows entering the aviary the maximum size should not be larger than ¾" (1.9cm), as they have an uncanny knack of finding their way in and consuming food, thereby leaving disease behind. The only slight disadvantage to such a mesh size is the aesthetic one of the wire being obtrusive; this can be reduced by painting it with black bitumen paint, this type of paint can be easily

13

applied by using a cheap foam decorating roller. Coating the wire with black bitumen has the advantage of increasing its life, and also allows one to see the birds more clearly. For those who wish to use traditional housing and require a mesh roof for the pen it is advisable to use some heavy gauge nylon or black polythene garden netting, or a type of the terylene game netting which is now available in a variety of gauges and mesh sizes. A word of caution regarding the garden netting made of polythene — some will become brittle when subjected to sunlight for any length of time. Black is preferable whatever the material. The advantage of using a soft type for the roof is that Partridge are inclined to fly up when frightened, and can easily scalp themselves if galvanised wire is used.

Designs

Before starting aviary construction, it is important to decide on the species you propose to keep. The main consideration is whether the aviary is to house a species which is totally hardy, needing a good shelter, but no heat, or one that requires limited heat in order to survive the winter. There are a number of designs which the aviculturist might like to consider, depending on his needs.

Design 'A' Partridge Pens

Some people prefer to see their birds housed at ground level with shrubs growing; this can be achieved by using this type of pen. A small flowering shrub or evergreen can be planted in the soil to the front of the pens, the floor then covered in 2" (50mm) of sand, kept clean and dry will prevent earthworms coming to the surface and being host to certain parasitic worms and incidental transporters of microbial diseases. If the pen is decorated with a few logs and some clean dried grass and leaves, the birds will soon feel at home, and when the breeding season comes around will be encouraged to make a natural nest, and if required, attempt to hatch and brood their own chicks. As the front of these pens is exposed to the elements, it is as well to arrange some sort of cover for the food dishes.

Design 'A' Typical Temperate Patridge Pen.

Design 'B' Aviaries

These were designed as a permanent structure, giving each pair of birds ample room to live as naturally as possible, being suitably planted with shrubs and grasses to resemble their natural habitat. At the end of each aviary there is a house in which the birds have their food and water; being raised off the ground they will also soon learn to roost in them.

Design 'C' Tropical House

This is a suitable type of accommodation for the less hardy species, originating from a tropical climate and not able to withstand the cold of European winters. It will also encourage such species to attempt to breed having provided a habitat similar to their own. In general the private aviculturist does not have access to a large tropical house as do Zoos or Wildlife Parks, therefore for economy reasons and to reduce the cost of heating, a smaller type of house is required and a further benefit to be obtained is that more than one pair of birds can be housed in a given area. In the house to be described there are three compartments which can house three species, each with its own territory which assists in giving a suitable habitat seclusion to achieve successful breeding.

General Construction

The Tropical House measures 12' x 8' (3.7m x 2.6m) and is constructed from ½" (25mm) chipboard or exterior plywood using 6' x 4' (1.8m x 1.2m) standard sheets, these are fixed to a 1¼" x 1¼" (32mm x 32mm) timber framework and bolted together forming the back and sides. A similar size framework is made for the roof on which is fixed corrugated polythene sheeting running from the front to the rear; on the underside of the framework is stretched a flat sheet of heavy gauge polythene to act as insulation and protection for the birds should they fly up. The front of the house is glazed three quarters of the way up, and has a fanlight type window runing the full length of the building to give ventilation during the summer months.

Partridge Pens

Design 'A'

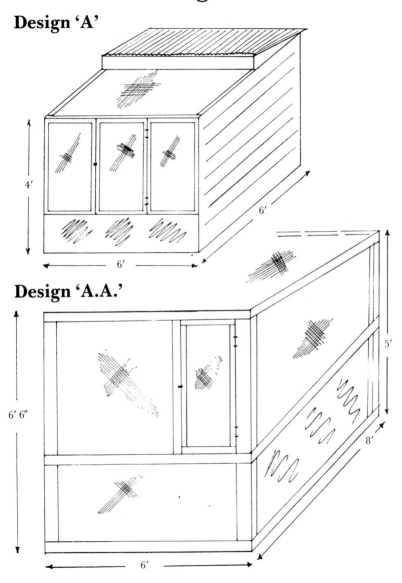

Design 'A.A.'

Design 'B'

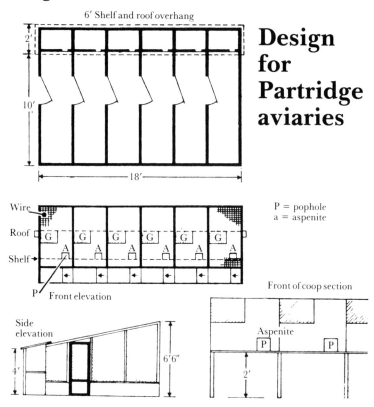

6' Shelf and roof overhang

2'

10'

18'

Design for Partridge aviaries

Wire
Roof
Shelf →
P / Front elevation

G G G G G G
A A A A A A

P = pophole
a = aspenite

Front of coop section

Side
elevation

4'

6'6"

Aspenite

P   P

2'

Design of a range of six Partridge Aviaries constructed by
Mr Keith Howman, of Shepperton, England.

Heating

A 3 Kw fan heater is installed behind a wire grill in the service area
within the house, being wired into a thermostat fixed some distance
away from the heater, but not in the direct line of the hot air. If
possible the temperature in summer should be kept around 70°F;
this seems to stimulate the urge to breed. In winter the temperature
is reduced to 55°F - 60°F for two reasons; the first to reduce the cost of

Tropical House

Design 'C'

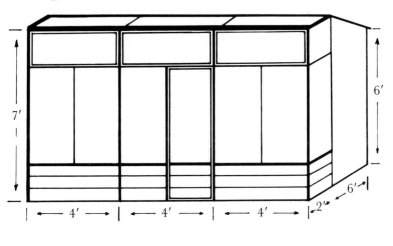

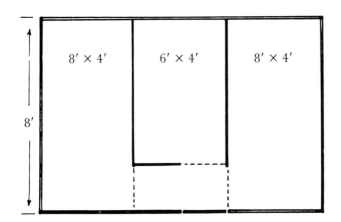

Plan View

heating, and the second to give the birds a rest from the breeding season.

Ventilation

The window running along the front of the house is opened automatically, using a greenhouse ventilator device which, expanding as the temperature rises above its base setting, pushes the window open, thus giving a circulation of air, and closes again as the temperature drops. In summer the same fan heater used during the winter can be switched to give cool air in the house, the fan being regulated by a second thermostat which cuts in when the temperature rises above 80°F. To achieve this it is best to have two outlet sockets each wired to its respective thermostat and the heater fitted with a plug, so the hot or cold air can be selected according to the season.

Floor Covering

To conserve moisture, a sheet of polythene is placed on the floor with its sides turned up approx 6″ (15cm) around the wall of each pen, then the floor is covered with at least 2″ (5cm) of sedge peat as used by gardeners to act as a base layer; this type of material is both clean and sterile. A further good layer of moss is added having been gathered from your local woods; this gives the Tropical House the type of floor covering which relates to the forest floor, and will encourage certain species such as Roulroul Partridge to nest. The next stage is to plant the house with a variety of plants to give the necessary cover to the birds and give the security needed for them to breed.

Suggested Plants

Maidenhair fern	*Adiantum capillis-veneris*
Tree ferns	*Cyathea* spp.
Filmy ferns	*Hymenophyllum* spp. (req. moist atmosphere)
Tree ferns	*Dicksonia* spp.
Small trailing Fig	*Ficus pumila*
Pink flowers	*Jasminum beesianum* (semi-evergreen climber)
Swiss cheese plant	*Monstera deliciosa* (huge leaves)

20

Passion fruit	*Passiflora* spp. (vig., semi-evergreen climber)
Trumpet vine	*Campsis radican*
Dwarf palm 4'	*Chamaerops humilis*
Figs	*Ficus elastica*
	Ficus benjamina
Pink flowers	*Indigofera gerardiana*
Banana	*Musa* spp.
White flowers	*Myrtus communis* (small evergreen leaves)
Avocado	*Persea gratissima* (grow from stone; large leaves)
Spiky Cactus	*Yucca* spp.

Watering System

With a planted aviary in a heated area, your plants need a fair amount of water to keep them fresh and to promote growth, but watering is a problem as your birds will not take kindly to your intrusion into their secluded area. It is therefore necessary to instal an overhead mist watering system, which will give a blanket of fine water droplets over the whole area. Your local garden centre can help you with this type of inexpensive equipment. The frequency of use depends on the season of the year and how hot it becomes during the day; during the winter you only need to switch on the system for perhaps 5 - 10 minutes once a week, but during the heat of the summer it can be switched on every three days for approximately the same period. The system is simply connected to your water tap as is a garden hose; you will be surprised how your birds enjoy the watering sessions, which can stimulate nesting activity in some species.

THE OVERHEAD MIST LINE
A Method of Controlling Humidity in Aviaries

Egg Collection

One is always faced with the problem of extracting eggs from an aviary without disturbing the birds, to overcome this a bamboo cane is used with a piece of heavy gauge wire bent into a ring of no more than 1″ (2.5cm) diameter attached to one end. This can then be slid under the egg and then lifted out without disturbance.

CHAPTER 3

GENERAL MANAGEMENT AND HUSBANDRY

Perhaps the most important aspect of keeping Partridge is their management, which means care and detail. Anyone can throw a handful of food into the aviary once a day and then clear off to work. The birds might well survive for a long time, but if you are keen to breed and raise the rarer species, it is necessary to take a little more care. As with a shepherd who knows each sheep by sight and its individual traits, the Partridge breeder should go to the same trouble and check each bird visually each day to see if it is still in good condition; a bird sitting in the corner looking miserable is the first sign that things are not right. Regular feeding is always recommended; some breeders prefer to feed daily rather than giving their birds food hoppers to feed on an ad lib basis. Personally, I have to feed all the adult stock by the ad lib principle for two reasons; one, to save time, and the other, to prevent hungry birds pecking at anything they come across, which could well be each other; that is not to say my birds are not checked every day.

To help the person who has not come across sickness in his birds before, listed below are the main common ailments likely to be encountered.

Common Ailments of Adult and Full-grown Birds

Infectious Sinusitus

Cause: Infection with various micro-organisms such as Mycoplasma with secondary infections with *E. coli*, Haemo-
philus and Staphylococcus.

Signs: Nasal discharge, together with swelling of the face due
to pus in the sinuses.

Treatment: Antibiotics can be useful (Tylan or Rovamycin). Multi-
vitamins including Vitamin A given on a regular basis
will help to strengthen the birds' resistance.

Chronic Respiratory Disease

Cause: Infection with virus or Mycoplasma. Secondary infection with other micro-organisms are usual. Aspergillosis due to the fungus *Aspergillus fumigatus* and ornithosis due to Chlamydia may show similarities to CRD.

Signs: Loss of appetite and depression are noticeable with a decline of body weight. There may be a nasal discharge and breathing difficulties.

Treatment: Use of antibiotics is the best treatment (Tylan, Rovamycin, Aureomycin), together with increased ventilation in their quarters.

Bronchitis and Pneumonia

Cause: Infection by many micro-organisms already listed including *Aspergillus fumigatus* and the parasitic gapeworm. In some cases the trouble may be precipitated by excess cold, draughts and subsequent chilling.

Signs: Laboured breathing, gaping with coughing and squeaking, or coughing with a head flick in the case of gapes — the so-called 'snicking'. Birds are inclined to stand with feather fluffed up holding their wings away from the body. Sinusitus may also be present.

Treatment: Isolate in a hospital pen at a temperature of 70°F - 75°F; inhalations of Friars Balsam could be of help. Specific antibiotics or drugs may be used with the approval of your vet.

Enteritis. Inflammation of the Intestine.

Cause: Ingestion of contaminated food or water, unsuitable foods, or specific infectious diseases, also can be associated with the micro-organism *E. coli* in the gut.

Signs: The affected bird shows excessive thirst and a craving for grit. Profuse greenish diarrhoea. The vent becomes stained and matted with droppings.

Treatment: Place in a hospital pen, at a temperature of 70°F - 80°F, with attention paid to diet. Antibiotics may be given (Neomycin and Streptomycin).

Blackhead

Cause: A protozoan disease which affects all types of game birds, transmitted by caecal worms.

Signs: An affected bird shows signs of lowered head and wings, drowsiness, ruffled feathers and a yellowish diarrhoea, although young birds may die without showing signs of the disease.

Treatment: Prevention is the best treatment; transferring the birds to clean ground. Affected birds can be treated with Emtryl, some compounded chick crumbs do include a minimal prevention dose of an anti-blackhead drug.

Coccidiosis

Cause: A protozoan disease that affects the blind-guts (caeca) and the intestines.

Signs: Affected birds may die unexpectedly when apparently in good condition, especially younger birds. Others show emaciation, anaemia, white or yellow diarrhoea, reduced appetite and thirst.

Treatment: Amprol-Plus Solution is the preferred treatment. Use for up to 2 weeks to allow an immunity to develop (graded dosing regime). Strict attention must be paid to diet and hygiene. Embazin may be used under the direction of your vet.

Scaly-Leg

Cause: By mites of the Cnemidocoptes species. Often from old bantams.

Signs: Scaliness of the legs, with a honeycomb appearance, nodular masses form around the legs.

Treatment: Acriflavine emulsion 1 part to 1,000 as an antiseptic applied daily for 2 weeks; Gamma B.H.C. 0.02% in soft paraffin.

(Note: These can be obtained combined as a yellow cream, acriflavine acting as a general antiseptic and the B.H.C. acting specifically on the mite.)

Aspergillosis

Cause: A particular fungus called *Aspergillus fumigatus*. Often a secondary problem in old birds.

Signs: None, laboured breathing and loss of weight.

Treatment: None. Prevent by avoiding accumulations of rotting vegetable matter. Old hay, straw or food are often sources.

Avian Tuberculosis

Cause: A resistant micro-organism that persists in the soil contaminated via droppings of sick birds.

Signs: Typical of 2nd year and older birds. Gradual wasting and development of weakness.

Treatment: None. Good hygiene and management goes a long way to preventing this disease. Pen young stock on clean ground, change soil, sand, etc., keep wild birds away from the tops of pens to reduce faecal contamination and use 'Ministry Approved' disinfectants suitable for TB.

Feather Lice, Mites and Fleas

Signs: Irritation and scratching, restlessness and ruffling of feathers.

Treatment: These parasites can be controlled by dusting the birds and their quarters with a proprietary dusting powder obtainable from most chemists and pet shops.

Newcastle disease or Fowl Pest

Cause: A virus disease found primarily in domestic poultry and certain wild birds.

Signs: In newly imported birds, sudden death without previous signs may be encountered; possibly difficult breathing, loss of use of legs and backward bending of head are noticeable.

Treatment: No treatment is possible. A notifiable disease in U.K. Contact your Vet immediately:

Worm Control

Worms live in the gut and other organs and their eggs are passed in the droppings. Generally worms cause a stunting of growth in young stock and adult birds become droopy. Treatment can be in the form of periodic worming medication in the feed or water.

Treatment: Thibenzole as per instructions; or Mebenvet at the rate of 1 oz per 6 lb of food for 14 days. To keep your birds in good condition a dose prior to and after the breeding season is recommended, but not during or two weeks before egg laying. Nemicide and Gapex are also valuable wormers in the appropriate circumstances.

Common Ailments of Chicks and Young Poults

The most troublesome ailment is probably coccidiosis which can be treated with Amprol Plus Solution. A coccidiostat should be present in the diet (ACS). Blackhead can be a problem but an anti-blackhead supplement (ABS) should help prevention. Aspergillosis affects all ages, but can be very serious in chicks, or even in the egg, where there is poor hatchery hygiene. Chilling, overheating, a reluctance to start feeding and drinking, and poor hygiene can lead to heavy losses often exacerbated by an *E. coli* infection. Gapes may be a problem after a few weeks where birds are reared on grass and have access to earthworms, slugs and other invertebrates.

Hexamitiasis/Trichomoniasis

Cause: Protozoans in the intestines and blind-guts.

Signs: Poor growth and food uptake. Thirst and fever. Copious yellow, frothy droppings. Mucky feathers, unpleasant sickly smell.

Treatment: Terramycin, Emtryl or Furasol. (The latter must be used with great care at half poultry rates.) Your Vet will prescribe and advise.

Prevention: Use high protein starter crumb for shorter period, rear on grass or with bantams, administer Vitamin C in drinking water (try 1 gram per gal.).

Vet's advice:

Should there be any doubt always consult your vet. In fact, you now have to obtain many of the drugs mentioned from him in the U.K., as they are no longer allowed to be sold on the open market. Therefore, providing your vet agrees, every breeder with more than a few pairs should keep a small drug cupboard stocked with the following for emergencies:

Mebenvet - as a wormer

Emtryl - against blackhead

Amprol-Plus Solution - against coccidiosis

Terramycin - as a broad spectrum antibiotic

Tylan - for sinusitis

Administration of Medicine

Always avoid handling your birds as, when they are off colour, they become very stressed. It is always better to administer drugs through their food or water, that is of course, providing they are not too sick to eat or drink.

Disinfection

Following any infectious disease, all houses and aviaries should be thoroughly disinfected with 'Ministry Approved' products and scrubbed with hot washing soda or Dettol at the rate of 1 in 20 solution. Should you decide to use Izal or Jeyes Fluid at the rate of 1 in 10 solution, care should be taken, as these fluids have a caustic action and could damage the feet of the birds unless perches etc. are well scrubbed with plain water after the soaking.

For open flights with natural earth or gravel base, the top soil or gravel should be removed and buried. Lime (1 lb per sq yard) should be applied and allowed to remain for one week. This should then be dug over and a new layer of soil or gravel placed on top. Birds should not be returned for at least one week after treatment.

CHAPTER 4

FEEDING

Diet for Your Adult Stock

We must first define the type of adult stock you are to feed and maintain in good condition ready for the breeding season. Basically, there are two types, Temperate and Tropical species: the first type covers all the Partridges from cold and temperate zones, which in turn are split into two groups — the game species which are bred for sporting purposes, and the subject of a separate chapter, and the remaining group, which by far represents the majority of the temperate species kept for conservation or ornamental purposes.

Temperate species

In most parts of the developed world today the aviculturist can obtain a compounded pellet which has been specially formulated to give all the necessary ingredients required by this type of partridge. The important thing to remember during the out of season months (non breeding) is that the pellet you feed must be of a low protein level and designed as a maintenance ration, whereas the breeders pellet has additional ingredients added to bring your birds into condition ready for egg laying. Some people prefer to give these pellets on an ad lib basis in some form of hopper, without any additional fare. However I believe it is helpful to give a mixture of small seed to supplement the diet, also some greenfood can be helpful if they are housed on sand and have no access to a grass aviary, Having said that, certain species are less inclined to eat greenfood than others — for guidance refer to the natural food requirement detailed against the species in chapter 5. Do not forget that when birds are kept in captivity they require a good supply of both limestone and flint grit, as it is of great help in grinding the food in the crop. Another important point is to have clean drinking water available at all times.

Referring to the types of pelleted food available, the following may be of help:

Partridge Breeders Pellets 17% protein level	Breeding
Partridge Poult Pellets 15%	Non-Breeding
Partridge Maintenance Pellets 13%	Non-Breeding
Partridge Growers Pellets 20%	Over 6 weeks
Partridge Chick Crumbs 24%	Over 14 days
Partridge Starter Crumbs 28%	First 14 days

(The above courtesy of Spratts Game Foods.)

Note: Certain of the smaller species may not be able to take a larger diameter pellet and may refuse to eat. Discuss the problem with your food supplier or mill and they may agree to make a smaller pellet for you (a mini pellet), or suggest an alternative food suitable for turkeys.

Tropical species

When trying to keep this type of bird in captivity one has to have far more imagination with their feeding requirements than with the previous group. Most of these birds originate from parts of the world where fruit, berries and insects form the major part of their diet, therefore due consideration must be given to this fact. To help the aviculturist overcome this problem an account of the food taken in the natural habitat is included with the information given against each species, where it is known, in chapter 5. Unfortunately there is very little written on how one can successfully maintain such species in captivity, possibly because only a very few have ever been kept and bred in confinement on a regular basis to date, and therefore it becomes very much trial and error in formulating a suitable diet. For a number of years we have kept Roulroul Partridge *Rollulus roulroul*, which are possibly the most commonly kept tropical partridge, and have found the following mixture very successful in maintaining and breeding this species :

  2 parts Java Dove Mixture
  1 part Poult or Breeders Pellets
  ½ part Insectile Mixture
  1 eggcupful of Sunflower seed oil

The above ingredients are well mixed in a bucket and finally sprinkled with a little vitamin additive, and then fed ad lib in a small dish each day. Also a small amount of chopped fruit is offered to those interested. You will find each species will pick out their requirements from the dish allowing one to determine the mixture they require to satisfy their needs. In addition it must be remembered to have fine mixed grit and clean water available at all times. As some of the food mentioned above is described by its brand name it might be useful to try and give the makeup of each.

Java Dove Mixture comprises:

Mixed Millets
Red and White Milo (Dari)
Pearl Barley
Cut Maize
Wheat
Canary Seed
Hemp Seed

Pellets

As already mentioned pellets are fed depending on the season, but with birds from the tropics the seasons are out of phase with those in Europe, and the best guide is to note the condition of your birds and feed Poult Pellets when they are in moult, returning to Breeders Pellets when you consider your stock in good enough condition to breed.

Insectile Mixture

Many brands are available suitable for various softbilled birds. This particularly covers species which rely on a high insectile diet. The ingredients are generally as follows:

Soya Flour
Fish Meal
Ground Shrimp
Meat and Bone Meal
Ground Flies
Hemp and Maw Seed
Biscuit Meal
Currants and Sultanas
All mixed with a little Honey

This type of food is very liable to go stale, therefore only mix or buy your requirements in small quantities.

When faced with feeding a new species you will find it best to allow them to select and eat what they require, and then adjust the total mix to take account of their needs, thus reducing the amount of waste. Some breeders will also offer chopped hard boiled eggs and chopped ox heart on occasion, but it is really up to the individual to decide on a balanced diet for his stock.

Live Food

Apart from the nutritional value of mealworms, they are extremely useful in taming down newly imported birds. They will soon come to expect a daily offering of a worm or two each day at feeding time.

Maggots are used on occasion, but not recommended; they can carry botulism and if used must be well cleaned in bran or sawdust for at least three to four days. In fact, their bodies must not show any colour inside before feeding. Maggots are usually obtained from a fishing shop, sold by the ounce. There are various types; the best called pinkies, a small pink maggot ideal because of its size. Mealworms are both the cleanest and most practical insect to feed, only requiring a few inches of bran to be maintained. Choose a container such as an aquarium to house them in, place layers of newspaper or sacking on top of the bran because the mealworms like getting between the layers and can be easily collected. The reproductive cycle of a mealworm is fairly slow and that is the reason why they are so expensive to buy. They can be obtained from either your pet shop or via one of the weekly avicultural newspapers.

Grit

Grit plays a major part in a bird's digestive system, being consumed and deposited in its gizzard; this grinds the food into a paste, allowing the food to be digested. There are two forms of grit, each having a different purpose; granite and flint for assisting digestion, and limestone and oyster shell, which is soluble, intended for laying birds and should be provided during the laying season to replace the calcium that goes into making the egg shells.

Food Additives

To bring breeding stock into condition and for healthy birds throughout the year, a vitamin-mineral supplement is essential. It

Chukar Partridge

Red-legged Partridge

Barbary Partridge

Richard Robjent 1982

Sand Partridge

See See Partridge

Rock Partridge

Richard Robjent 1982

Boulton's Hill Partridge

White-throated Hill Partridge

Brown-breasted Hill Partridge

Richard Robje

Black Wood Partridge

Rickett's Hill Partridge

Hainun Hill Partridge

Richard Robjen

should be sprinkled onto the food at a rate of one teaspoonful per 8 birds. It is true that most compounded pelleted food is formulated to give the required vitamins and minerals, but in practice I have found the additional vitamins and minerals included within the modern supplement are of benefit and well worth using, giving the adult stock the extra trace factors to produce sound progeny.

Vitamins and their use

Vitamin A	for resistance to disease and formation of bones
Vitamin B1 (Thiamine Mononitrate Sup.)	for healthy nervous system, appetite and digestion.
Vitamin B2 (Riboflavine BP) Nicotinic Acid BP }	for optimal growth and function of all body cells.
Vitamin B6 (Pyridoxine Hydrochloride BP)	for metabolism of proteins.
Vitamin B12 (Cyanocobalamin EP)	for promotion of growth and improved hatchability of eggs.
Calcium Pantothenate USP	for good feather development, growth and appetite
Folic Acid BP	essential to growth, reproduction and normal feathering.
Choline Chloride	to help in metabolism of dietary fats.
Vitamin E	for normal reproduction and muscle development.
Menadione USNF	for production of prothrombin, the anthaemorrhagic factor in the blood.

The above are found in a vitamin supplement called 'Vionate' manufactured by E. R. Squibb and Sons Ltd., Animal Health Divn., Regal House, Twickenham Middlesex, England.

CHAPTER 5

PARTRIDGE SPECIES

As with Quail, there has been very little written giving a complete list of Partridge found throughout the world; with this in mind a comprehensive list has been prepared from the checklist given in *A Complete Checklist of the Birds of the World* by Richard Howard and Alick Moore, Oxford Press 1980. With this basic information on each species, additional data has also been included, such as any sub-species known, natural habitat, food, and distribution in the world. Where possible a clear description is given of each species, together with avicultural notes for those partridge known to be kept in captivity.

Species for the Beginner

Certain species have been kept in captivity for many years, and become accustomed to a semi-domesticated environment. The Red-legged Partridge *Alectoris rufa* and the Grey Partridge *Perdix perdix* are possibly the best species for the novice to start with, progressing later to the rarer species. In the avicultural notes against each species an indication has been given regarding its suitability for the beginner.

Purchase of Stock

Below are some basic rules which are well worth considering when purchasing stock.

a) Too often birds are offered for sale as a true pair, with a complete disregard of the fact that they may be brother and sister; if this practice continues there will be a genetic decline of the species. Therefore it is essential that unrelated stock is obtained.

b) Try and buy the cock and hen from different sources — this always sounds easier than it is in practice. Most breeders are reluctant to sell only a hen bird, leaving a surplus of cocks at the end of the season, therefore always buy the hen bird first.

c) Only buy from a breeder of repute.

d) A failsafe method is to buy two pairs of the same species from different sources, then swap the cock birds over. The surplus pair can then be sold as unrelated, or kept as an insurance.

e) Young birds should always be purchased fully feathered and not minus tail or back feathers, due to feather pecking. Birds denuded of feathers cannot be expected to survive outdoor conditions in the way a normal feathered bird can — so if you have the chance, see the birds before accepting delivery.

Ref. Phasianidae	**Partridge**
1. *Alectoris graeca*	Rock Partridge
2. *chukar*	Chukar Partridge
3. *magna*	Przewalski Rock Partridge
4. *philbyi*	Philby's Rock Partridge
5. *barbara*	Barbary Partridge
6. *rufa*	Red-legged Partridge
7. *melanocephala*	Arabian Chukar Partridge
8. *Ammoperdix griseogularis*	See See Partridge
9. *heyi*	Sand Partridge
10. *Arborophila torqueola*	Common Hill Partridge
11. *rufogularis*	Rufous-throated Hill Partridge
12. *atrogularis*	White-cheeked Hill Partridge
13. *crudigularis*	White-throated Hill Partridge
14. *mandellii*	Red-breasted Hill Partridge
15. *brunneopectus*	Brown-breasted Hill Partridge
16. *rufipectus*	Boulton's Hill Partridge
17. *gingica*	Rickett's Hill Partridge
18. *davidi*	David's Tree Partridge
19. *cambodiana*	Chestnut-headed Tree Partridge
20. *orientalis*	Sumatran Hill Partridge
21. *javanica*	Chestnut-bellied Tree Partridge
22. *rubrirostris*	Red-billed Tree Partridge
23. *hyperythra*	Red-breasted Tree Partridge
24. *ardens*	Hainan Hill Partridge
25. *Bambusicola fytchii*	Bamboo Partridge
26. *thoracica*	Chinese Bamboo Partridge
27. *Caloperdix oculea*	Ferruginous Wood Partridge

28.	*Haematortyx sanguiniceps*	Crimson-headed Wood Partridge
29.	*Lerwa lerwa*	Snow Partridge
30.	*Margaroperdix madagascariensis*	Madagascar Partridge
31.	*Melanoperdix nigra*	Black Wood Partridge
32.	*Perdix perdix*	Grey Partridge
33.	*dauricae*	Daurian Partridge
34.	*hodgsoniae*	Tibetan Partridge
35.	*Ptilopachus petrosus*	Stone Partridge
36.	*Rhizothera longirostris*	Long-billed Wood Partridge
37.	*Rollulus roulroul*	Crested Wood Partridge
38.	*Tetragallus caucasicus*	Caucasian Snowcock
39.	*caspius*	Caspian Snowcock
40.	*tibetanus*	Tibetan Snowcock
41.	*altaicus*	Altai Snowcock
42.	*himalayensis*	Himalayan Snowcock
43.	*Tetraophasis obscurus*	Verreaux's Monal Partridge
44.	*szechenyii*	Szechenyi's Monal Partridge
45.	*Tropicoperdix charltonii*	Chestnut-breasted Tree Partridge
46.	*chloropus*	Green-legged Hill Partridge
47.	*merlini*	Annamese Hill Partridge

Rock Partridge
Ref. 1.

Alectoris graeca
(Meisner 1804)

Sub-species

A.g. graeca	- S.E. Europe
A.g. saxatilis	- Alps
A.g. whitakeri	- Sicily

Distribution
South Eastern Europe

Habitat
Rocky, stony and thinly grassed hills and mountain slopes, vineyards.

Food
Mainly plants, shoots, seeds and fruit

Description
Adults. 13" (33cm). Sexes alike. Very similar to the Chukar *A. chukar* by noticeable clean head and throat, cleaner and sharper face and throat pattern, greyer chest and upper parts, and sharper pattern of the narrower flank bars. Rufous corners of the tail always obvious against pale underparts. No seasonal variations. Male slightly larger.

Avicultural Notes	Temperate
Recommended size of aviary	Minimum size 6' x 6' (2m x 2m)
Numbers in captivity	54 - 1978, 276 - 1982, W.P.A. Census.
Egg colour	Oval, smooth and glossy, yellow-cream or pale buff, lightly to heavy speckled red-brown.
Egg clutch size	8 - 14 eggs
Incubation period	24 - 26 days
Noise level	Reasonable
Habits	Ground dwelling
Food	Pellets, mixed corn and millet.
Novice selection	Rare in captivity

Chukar Partridge
Ref. 2.

Alectoris chukar
(J.E. Grey 1830)

Sub-species

A.c. kleini	- E. Greece
A.c. cypriotes	- Cyclades, Asia Minor
A.c. kurdistanica	- S. Kurdistan
A.c. chukar	- Himalayas
A.c. potanni	- W. Mongolia
A.c. pubescens	- S. Manchuria, N. China

Distribution
Cyprus, Southern Turkey, Eastern Greece, South Kurdistan, Himalayas through to North China.

Habitat
Scree slopes with bushes and trees down to dry valleys and sometimes arable fields.

Food
Mainly seed, grasses and weeds, to a lesser extent insects.

Description
Adults. 13″ (33cm). Sexes alike. A rotund medium sized gamebird. Male grey-brown, nape and underparts grey-brown. Scapulars pale blue with rufous margins. Supercilium, lores and cheeks yellow-white, chin, throat and upper neck pale yellow-buff. Thin black frontal band and eye stripe extend into necklace around throat, widening on foreneck. Eye stripe interrupted with rufous behind the eye. Dark speckles above centre of necklace unique to this species. Chest grey, flanks basically white, barred vertically with 9 - 10 black and chestnut lines. Iris, light brown to brown. Bill, light clean red. Legs, coral red. Female smaller, with less distinct head and neck pattern and slightly duller plumage.

Avicultural Notes

	Temperate
Recommended size of aviary	Minimum size 6′ x 6′ (2m x 2m)
Numbers in captivity	Bred in quantity for sporting purposes.
Egg colour	Oval, smooth and glossy, cream or pale buff, variably spotted

	red-brown (39mm x 30mm).
Egg clutch size	8 - 15 eggs
Incubation period	22 - 24 days
Noise level	Reasonable
Habits	Ground dwelling
Food	Pellets, corn/millet. Little green food.
Novice selection	Possible.

Przewalski Rock Partridge

Alectoris magna

Great Partridge

(Przewalski 1876)

Ref. 3.

Sub-species

A.m. magna   - E. Tibet, W. Kansu

Distribution

Eastern Tibet, West China.

Habitat

Mountain slopes, stony hillsides.

Food

Shoots, seeds, insects.

Description

Adults. 15″ (38.1cm). Sexes alike. Generally similar to *A. chukar*, a more robust body, has a double collar with black on the inside, reddish-brown on the underside and rump, a finer barring on the flanks, but spaced farther apart.

Avicultural Notes   Temperate

None recorded.

Philby's Rock Partridge

Alectoris philbyi

Ref. 4.

(Lowe 1934)

Sub-species

A.p. philbyi   - SW Arabia

Distribution
South West Arabia, Yemen.
Habitat
Rock and stony hillsides, Range up to 1,000 feet.
Food
Seed, berries, plant shoots and insects.
Description
Adults. 15" (38.1cm). Sexes alike. Whole top of head dull blue-grey with slight brownish wash, whole upper parts and breast dark vinous brown, abdomen cinnamon, flanks boldly barred black, white and chestnut, line above the eye whitish, chin, cheeks and throat black, spotted cinnamon on lower throat. Bill, feet, and eye-ring dull coral red.
Avicultural Notes   Temperate
None Recorded.

Barbary Partridge   *Alectoris barbara*
Ref. 5.   (Bonnaterra 1790)

Sub-species	
A.b. barbara	- N. Morocco, N. Algeria, Tunisia
A.b. theresae	- S. Morocco
A.b. koenigi	- Canary Is.
A.b. spatzi	- S. Algeria, S. Tunisia
A.b. barbata	- Libya

Distribution
Northeast Morocco, Northern Algeria, Northern Tunisia, Sardinia, Libya, Canary Is.
Habitat
Bare stony hills in scrub or woodland up to altitudes of 10,000 feet. Sparse bushes on sandy coastal hills, coastal sand dunes, wadis with dry tree cover.
Food
Seeds, shoots, young leaves, possibly insects.

Description

Adults. 13" (33cm). Crown, nape and collar on lower neck deep chestnut, last nearly black at sides with white spots, rest of upper parts grey-brown, vinaceous wash. Scapular slate-blue with wide rufous margins, as in the Chukar *A. chukar*. Long supercilium, lores, cheeks and throat pale grey. Pink-chestnut eyestripe, overlaid with long orange-buff feathers behind the eye, extends to join collar. Chest pink-grey. Flanks basically pale slate, overlaid with bars of black, sandy-buff or white. Buff on front of belly and vent more obvious than on other *Alectoris*. Male slightly larger than female. Iris, light brown or red-brown. Bill, crimson or orange-red. Legs, strawberry-red.

Avicultural Notes	Temperate
Recommended size of aviary	Minimum size 6' x 6' (2m x 2m)
Numbers in captivity	50 - 1978., 127 - 1982. W.P.A. Census
Egg colour	Oval, smooth and slightly glossy, very pale yellow-buff, finely marked red-brown
Egg clutch size	10 - 14 eggs
Incubation period	25 days
Noise level	Can be loud
Habits	Ground dwelling
Food	Pellets, corn, millet.
Novice selection	Possible.

Red-legged Partridge
French Partridge
Ref. 6.

Alectoris rufa

Sub-species	
A.r. rufa	- S.E. Europe
A.r. hispanica	- N.W. Spain & N. Portugal
A.r. intercedens	- S. Spain
A.r. corsa	- Corsica
A.r. australis	- Gran Canaria Is.

Distribution
Western Europe, from south and south western France to the north western tip of Italy, Corsica, Gran Canaria Is.
Habitat
Scrub in lowlands, hills, dry meadows, heathland and cultivated areas.
Food
Grass seeds, grain, fruits, berries, plant material.
Description
Adults. 13½" (34.3cm). Upper parts chestnut brown, shading to grey on the crown, cheeks and throat whote, bordered by a black band, white stripe above eyes, skin around eye red, breast blue-grey, flanks barred white, black and chestnut, belly and under-tail rufous. Bill, red. Legs, red.

Avicultural Notes

	Temperate
Recommended size of aviary	Minimum size 6' x 6' (2m x 2m)
Numbers in captivity	Bred in large numbers for sporting purposes.
Egg colour	Buff with dark brown spots.
Egg clutch size	9 - 12 eggs (two clutches laid by each hen, then each incubated by cock and hen of the pair).
Incubation period	18 - 21 days
Noise level	Reasonable
Habits	Ground dwelling
Food	Pellets, grain, millet. Green food
Novice selection	Good.

Arabian Chukar
Alectoris melanocephala

Ref. 7.

Sub-species

A.m. melanocephala.	- S.W. Arabia
A.m. guichardi	- E. Hadhramaut

Distribution
Arabia, from Jeddah in Saudi Arabia to Muscat in Oman.

Habitat
   Rocky hillside amongst grass and bush.
Food
   Seeds, corn, grass, and weeds.
Description
   Adults. 12½" - 14½" (31.7cm - 36.8cm). Forehead to nape streak
   under eye, patch behind ear coverts and 'v' shaped collar on sides
   of neck meeting at the front, black; stripe over eye; cheeks, chin
   and throat white; ear coverts streaked black and white; sides of
   neck pale brown; chest, flanks and tail pale grey; bill red. Note
   female lacks spurs.
Avicultural Notes   **Temperate**
   Thought to be the same as *Alectoris chukar.*

See See Partridge   *Ammoperdix griseogularis*
Ref. 8.   (Brandt 1843)

   Sub-species
   A.g. griseogularis   - S. Russia, Iran to N.W. India
   A.g. peraticus   - W. Afghanistan

Distribution
   Afghanistan, Iran, Northwest India, South Borneo.
Habitat
   Foothills of arid or semi-arid mountains and hills, or in semi-
   deserts within altitude of 100 - 2000 metres.
Food
   Seed, plant material, insects (ants, beetles, flies).
Description
   Adults. 9½" (24.1cm). Mainly grey-brown, faintly spotted and
   barred on underparts and wings. Head basically grey with broad
   black forecrown extending into supercilium contrasting with
   long diamond shaped white eye stripe (narrowly bordered black
   below) and grey cheeks and throat. Neck and chest vinous-buff
   with pink-grey patch near shoulder extending back as base
   colour to flanks. Flanks strongly striped with 5 - 6 curving lines of
   black and pink-chestnut. Underbody cream, but undertail buff.

Female. Plumage uniform and sandier than male, on some the head and neck sides contains small dull white spots. Female, lacks spurs.

Female lacks spurs.

Avicultural Notes	Temperate
Recommended size of aviary	Minimum size 6' x 6' (2m x 2m)
Numbers in captivity	4 -1978, 5 - 1982, W.P.A. Census
Egg colour	Oval, smooth and glossy, pale buff to creamy-white or yellow
Egg clutch size	8 - 12 eggs (34.8 x 25.5mm).
Incubation period	21 days
Noise level	Reasonable
Habits	Ground dwelling. Males are pugnacious especially in breeding season.
Food	Pellets, millet, live food.
Novice selection	Not recommended

Sand Partridge
Ref. 9.

Ammopadix heyi
(Temminck 1825)

Sub-species	
A.h. heyi	- Jordan to Sinai
A.h. nicolli	- N. Egypt
A.h. cholmleyi	- River Nile to Red Sea
A.h. intermedia	- S. Arabia

Distribution
Israel, Jordan, Sinai, Saudi Arabia, North Egypt, Aden, Muscat.

Habitat
Hot desert or semi-desert, on steep rocky slopes, with sparse vegetation but access to water, will feed in rocky and sandy bottoms of steep-sided wadis.

Food
Seeds, berries, bulbs, plant material and insects.

Description

Adults. 8½" - 9¼" (21.7cm - 23.5cm). Male. Plumage basically vinous with obvious plumage pattern only on head and flanks, except for grey tone on head. Thin frontal band over base of bill to eye pale chestnut; back, wing, and centre of tail tinged brown and closely barred grey; flanks appear pink-grey, striped laterally with black and chestnut; outer tail feathers red-brown; bill, dull orange, chrome orange, or orange. Female, sandier and greyer, lacking pale patch on ear coverts. Bill, yellow-horn or dull yellow. In both, legs dull yellow or yellow.

Avicultural Notes	Temperate
Recommended size of aviary	Minimum size 6' x 6' (2m x 2m)
Numbers in captivity	22 - 1978, 6 - 1982, W.P.A. Census
Egg colour	Oval, smooth and glossy, pale sandy-buff, sometimes with grey or pink tint.
Egg clutch size	5 - 7 eggs (37mm x 27mm)
Incubation period	21 days
Noise level	Reasonable
Habits	Agile climber and runner
Food	Pellets, mixed millets, some green food, and mealworms.
Novice selection	Not suitable.

Common Hill Partridge

Arborophila torqueola
(Valenciennes 1826)

Ref. 10.

a) Simla Hill Partridge
b) Assam Hill Partridge
c) Kachin Hill Partridge

Sub-species

A.t. torqueola	- N.E. India, S. Tibet
A.t. millardi	- a) N.W. India
A.t. batemani	- b) Punjab, Himalayas and

	Himachal Pradesh
A.t. griseata	- c) N. Burma, N.W. Vietnam
A.t. interstinota	- N.W. Vietnam

Distribution
Himalayas from Garhwal to Nepal, north Burma, northwest Vietnam, south Tibet.

Habitat
Hillsides and ravines clad in dense forest, banj oak, laurel and evergreen trees and shrubs.

Food
Berries, seed, insects, grubs and shoots, together with tiny molluscs.

Description
Adults. 11″ (28cm). Sexes very similar, see below. Short-tailed, dumpy olive-brown partridge. Crown and nape bright chestnut, with the nape also spotted with black, narrow forehead and broad supercilium black. A black spotted chestnut line under supercilium, cheeks black, ear coverts bright chestnut, bare crimson skin around the eye, upperparts golden olive-brown finely barred with black and broadly mottled with chestnut and black. Chin, throat and neck black. Remainder of underparts grey and white with broad chestnut streaks and white drops on flanks, vent rufous-white with black bars, under tail coverts black and white. Eyes, brown to crimson-brown, bill, dark brown to black, legs and feet, olive-brown to grey. Female, crown brown, streaked with black, chin and throat rufous, spotted with black, breast brownish, separated from the throat by a chestnut band instead of white.

Sub-species

A.t. torqueola	breast brownish, crown olive-brown with white spots, abdomen pure white.
A.t. batemani	breast grey, crown chestnut, no chestnut on sides of neck
A.t. millardi	Abdomen rufescent

A.t. interstinta	Abdomen rufous richer and darker

Avicultural Notes	**Temperate**
Recommended size of aviary	Minimum size 6' x 6' (2m x 2m)
Numbers in captivity	10 - 1978, 42 - 1982, W.P.A. Census.
Egg colour	Pure, china white, glossy with a fine texture
Egg clutch size	3 - 5 eggs, up to a total of 9 (captive)
Incubation period	24 days
Noise level	Reasonable
Habits	Normally ground dwelling, but will perch to roost
Food	Pellets, mixed millets. Mealworm or two
Novice selection	Not recommended

Rufous-Throated Hill Partridge *Arborophila rufogularis*
Ref. 11. (Blyth 1850)

a) Arakan Hill Partridge

Sub-species

A.n. rufugularis	- N. India
A.n intermedia	- a) Assam to N.W. Burma
A.n tickelli	- S. Burma to S.W. Laos
A.n cinoa	- S. China, N. Laos
A.n. guttata	- C. Vietnam
A.n. annamensis	- S. Vietnam

Distribution
North India, southwest China, Burma, northwest Thailand, central south Annam, northwest Tonkin, north and central Laos, central south Vietnam.

Habitat
Heavy undergrowth in evergreen hill forest and dense secondary scrub on abandoned cultivation.
Food
Seed, berries, root shoots, insects and small molluscs.
Description
Adults. 10½" (26.7cm). Sexes very similar. Short tailed dumpy olive-brown partridge. Forehead grey, brown olive-brown stippled with black, long supercilium greyish white, sides of face white, speckled with black except on white moustachial stripe running from lower mandible to below dark brown ear coverts. Small naked red patch round eye, upperparts golden olive-brown, spotted with black on rump and upper tail coverts, scapulars and wing coverts chestnut and large grey and black drops, chin, throat, and sides of neck rufous, spotted with black. A broad band of ferruginous-red with a narrow black line below it separating foreneck from slatey grey breast. Anterior flanks slatey grey broadly streaked with deep orange-chestnut and with white drops, rear flanks brown with black crescentic spots. Female. Has fewer black spots on chin and throat and more white drops on breast and abdomen. Eyes, brown or red-brown, ocular skin pinkish-red or dull crimson, bill, dark brown, legs, and feet, pinkish-red to coral-red, claws, horny.

Avicultural Notes — Temperate

Recommended size of aviary	Minimum size 6' x 6' (2m x 2m)
Numbers in captivity	1 - 1978, 5 - 1982, W.P.A. Census.
Egg colour	Glossy china white
Egg clutch size	4 - 5 eggs (wild)
Incubation period	20 - 21 days
Noise level	Loud - ringing cry repeated
Habits	Basically ground dwelling
Food	Pellets, mixed millets, few mealworms
Novice selection	Not recommended

Common Hill Partridge

Female   Male

Male   Female

Crested Wood Partridge

Male   Female

Typical domed nest.

Green-legged Hill Partridge

Bamboo Partridge   Paintings By H Grönvold.

Red-Breasted Hill Partridge

Long-billed Wood Partridge

Rufous-throated Hill Partridge

Paintings By H Grönvold.

Snow Partridge

Red-breasted Tree Partridge

Daurian Partridge

White Cheeked Hill Partridge   *Arborophila atrogularis*
Ref. 12.   (Blyth 1850)
   Sub-species
   None known

Distribution
   Assam, southeast Asia, resident up to 4,000 ft in west, north and
   east Burma.
Habitat
   Scrub adjoining forest areas, near to wet undergrowth in less
   dense evergreen forest.
Food
   Seeds, shoots, berries, insects and grubs, also tiny molluscs.
Description
   Adults. 11″ (28cm). A dumpy, short-tailed olive-brown forest
   partridge. Males: Bill black. legs and feet dull orange to bright
   orange-red. Females: Bill dark brown,legs and feet dull wax
   yellow to yellow tinged with red. Forehead and supercilium grey;
   crown olive-brown, nape rufous, broadly spotted black. A black
   line below supercilium from lower to above cheeks, cheeks
   white, running behind into rufous buff ear coverts. Upperparts
   light olive-brown stippled and barred with black; scapular region
   barred amd mottled with black and white into grey breast and
   flanks. Flank grey, without any chestnut marks but with white
   dropping to the rear; tail coverts rufescent, edged with white,
   spotted with black. Eyes, brown or red-brown.

Avicultural Notes	Temperate
Recommended size of aviary	Minimum size 6′ x 6′ (2m x 2m)
Numbers in captivity	Nil recorded. W.P.A. Census.
Egg colour	China white.
Egg clutch size	3 - 7 eggs (wild).
Incubation period	Thought to be 20 - 21 days
Noise level	Reasonable
Habits	Ground dwelling
Food	Pellets, mixed millets, few mealworms.
Novice Selection	Not recommended.

49

White-Throated Hill Partridge

Arborophila crudigularis
(Swinhoe 1864)

Ref. 13.

Formosan Hill Partridge.

Distribution

Formosa, Taiwan.

Habitat

Mountains of interior, forest areas.

Food

Seeds, berries, young shoots, insects.

Description

Adults. 9½" (24.1cm). Sexes alike. Very similar colour to *A. atrigularis,* the back has a wider and darker barring; the chin, upper part of throat and foreneck are white, and the lower part of the throat black.

Avicultural Notes

	Temperate
Recommended size of aviary	Minimum size 6' x 6' (2m x 2m)
Numbers in captivity	12 - 1978, 44 - 1982, W.P.A. Census.
Egg colour	Glossy white, broad oval shape.
Egg clutch size	4 - 6 eggs
Incubation period	Thought to be 20 - 21 days
Noise level	Reasonable
Habits	Mainly ground dwelling, will scratch for food.
Food	Pellets, mixed millets, corn, mealworm or two.
Novice selection	Not suitable.

Red-Breasted Hill Partridge

Arborophila Mandellii
(Hume 1874)

Ref. 14.

Sub-species

None known

Distribution

Sikkim to east Assam, southeast Tibet.

Habitat
   Dense undergrowth in evergreen forest at an altitude of between
   350 and 2,450 metres.
Food
   Seeds, fruit, grubs and various insect life.
Description
   Adults. 11″ (28cm). Sexes alike. Typical dumpy hill partridge.
   Crown and nape dull chestnut-brown, dark grey superciliar
   stripes from eyes to behind, meeting on upper hindneck. A small
   moustachial streak lower hindneck and upper back reddish-
   chestnut with black spots. Upperparts olive, spotted and narrowly scalloped with black, chin and throat, pale olive-chestnut
   separated from deep chestnut upper breast by a double gorget
   of black and white, lower breast to vent grey marked on flanks
   with chestnut and white, undertail coverts olive with white spots
   and rufous mottling. Eyes, brown to red-brown, bill, black, legs
   and feet, reddish.

Avicultural Notes	Cold
Recommended size of aviary	Minimum size 6′ x 6′ (2m x 2m)
Numbers in captivity	Nil - 1978, 2 - 1982, W.P.A. Census.
Egg colour	China white.
Egg clutch size	4 - 6 eggs
Incubation period	Thought to be 20 - 21 days
Noise level	Loud, long drawn-out call.
Habits	Will roost in low bushes a few feet off the ground.
Food	Pellets, mixed millets, few mealworms.
Novice selection	Not recommended.

Brown-breasted Hill Partridge *Arborophila brunneopectus*
Ref. 15.   (Blyth 1855)

   Bare-Throated Tree Partridge

Bar-Backed Partridge
Sub-species
A.b. brunneopectus - E. Assam, S. Yunnan to S. Thailand.
A.b. henrici - N. & C. Vietnam.
A.b. albigula - S. Vietnam.

Distribution
Northern and central south Vietnam, northwest and southwest Thailand, Annam, Tonkin, Laos, south and east Burma, Malaysia.

Habitat
Broken ground in deep forests, generally at altitudes up to 4,500 feet.

Food
Seeds, insects, and small molluscs.

Description
Adults. 11″ (28 cm). Upper parts similar to *A. rufogularis*, but barred closely all over with black; feathers of throat and foreneck white or buffy white, with black tips; remaining underparts bright buff, whitish on belly, and barred black and white on sides. (Malaysian race has head, neck and throat mostly black with white cheeks and sides of forehead and white streaks on lower throat, rest of underparts grey, with black and rufous-buff bars on flanks and whitish centre of belly.

Avicultural Notes   Temperate
None Recorded

Boulton's Hill Partridge
Ref. 16.
Sub-species
None known

Arborophila rufipectus
(Boulton 1932)

Distribution
W. Szechwan, China.

Habitat

Forested terrain.

Food

Seed, and insects.

Description

Adults. 11″ (28 cm). Forehead whitish running into black striping on the crown and nape of the neck. Black in front, above and below the eye, with light chestnut patch behind the eye extending down to the upper back. White chin and throat flecked with black, upper back and rump dark brown with a band extending across lower breast, wings and tail brown, mottled with grey, lower breast white. Bill, black, legs, dark grey.

Avicultural Notes   Cold

None Recorded

Rickett's Hill Partridge   *Arborophila gingica*

Ref. 17.   (Gmelin 1788)

Distribution

Fukien, Kwengtung, 700 - 900 metres, - China.

Habitat

Hill country in densely wooded parts.

Food

Seed, berries, vegetable matter.

Description

Adults. 10″ (25 cm). Heavier proportions than Bamboo partridge but shorter in length. Forehead and crown greyish-fuscous, more or less streaked and mottled forward, and very noticeably from region above and behind eye to nape. Throat rich golden-rufous, slightly streaked dusky, the colour extending as a broad collar around base of neck where it is heavily mottled and streaked with black. Mantle and entire upperparts soft greyish with slight inclination to being pencilled in some specimens and with a slight rufous wash. Scapulars from shoulders very broadly and alternately marked grey and rufous to chestnut with dusky borders to the latter markings, the colours changing to regular and well defined markings on the coverts. Primaries dusky, washed with rufous, upper breast black to sides of nape, a rich and prominent crescent shaped bar of white separating the black from the chestnut colour of the breast, sides of breast, lower breast and underparts grey, lighter below, flanks mottled boldly with chestnut. Legs and feet, purplish-red. Female, similar to male, but more modestly marked.

Avicultural Notes	Temperate
Recommended size of aviary	Minimum size 6' x 6' (2m x 2m)
Numbers in captivity	Nil - 1978 and 1982, W.P.A. Census.
Egg colour	Whitish to olive-drab colour, pyriform shape
Egg clutch size	5 - 7 eggs (wild)
Incubation period	Not known
Noise level	Low whistling call
Habits	Thought to be ground dwelling
Food	Suggest mixed millets, pellets, as basic diet.
Novice selection	Not suitable - rare

David's Tree Partridge
Orange-necked Partridge
Ref. 18.

Arborophila davidi
(Delacour 1927)

Distribution
Central chain in the district of Bien Hoa, South Vietnam.
Habitat
Forest areas.
Food
Not known.
Description
Adults. 11" (28cm). Upperparts similar to *A. brunneopectus*; a white stripe extends from above eye to ear coverts, becoming rufous down sides of neck; black stripes through eye extends down sides of neck to join black breast band; throat rufous, chin white, breast brown flecked with black; lower breast, belly and flanks grey with strongly marked black feathers tipped with white on

flanks. Bill, black, feet, pinkish.

Avicultural Notes   Temperate
    None recorded

Chestnut-headed Tree Partridge *Arborophila cambodiana*
Ref. 19.   (Riley 1930)

Sub-species
A.c. cambodiana   - Cambodia
A.c. diversa   - S.E. Thailand

Distribution
    Cambodia, southest Thailand.
Habitat
    Mountainous forested areas.
Food
    Seeds, insects, and vegetable matter.
Description
    Adults. 11" (28cm). Male. Forehead and crown dark brown
    merging into rich chestnut above and below the eye, throat and
    breast, black stripe behind the eye. Upper back black running
    into rufous and slate grey wings and tail, interspersed with black,
    lower breast buff with black and white feathers at random.
    Female. Smaller. Lighter face colours, lower breast flecked with
    white feathers, upperparts, back and rump dark brown mottled
    with black. Bill, black, legs, reddish-brown.
Avicultural Notes   Temperate
    None recorded

Sumatran Hill Partridge   *Arborophila orientalis*
    Horsfield's Tree Partridge   (Horsfield 1822)
    Campbell's Tree Partridge
Ref. 20.

Sub-species
A.o. *campbelli*   - Malaysia
A.o. *rolli*   - N.W. Sumatra
A.o. *sumatrana*   - C. Sumatra
A.o. *orientalis*   - E. Java

Distribution
Malaysia, Sumatra, Java.
Habitat
Gullies and river valleys at 4,000' - 5,000', overgrown areas with slender rotans.
Food
Fruits, insects, and small snails.
Description
Adults. 11" (28cm). General description seems to be similar to *Arborophila j. javanica.* Could well be sub-species.

Avicultural Notes	Tropical
Recommended size of aviary	Minimum size 6' x 6' (2m x 2m)
Numbers in captivity	None recorded in 1978 and 1982, W.P.A. Census.
Egg colour	Pure white and somewhat glossy
Egg clutch size	2 eggs (wild)
Incubation period	Not known
Noise level	Suggested low call
Habits	Ground dwelling
Food	Tropical partridge mixture, fruit, live food.
Novice selection	Not suitable

Chestnut-Bellied Tree Partridge
Arborophila javanica
(Brown 1776)
Javan Tree Partridge
Bare-Throated Tree Partridge
Ref. 21.
Sub-species
A.j. *javanica*   - W. Java
A.j. *bartelsi*   - C. Java

A.j. *lawuana*   - C. Java
A.j. *rolli*   - Sumatra*

*J. Delacour, *Birds of Malaysia*, placed these a sub-species of *A. brunneopectus*

Distribution
Java, Sumatra.

Habitat
Mountians of Java, montane forest above 3,500 feet.

Food
Seeds, insects.

Description
Adults. 11″ (28cm). Head and neck black with white patches above and below the red skin around the eye; a broken collar of white and some red marks on the throat; upperparts including tail olive-brown, barred with black; wings chestnut and black browner at the edges; underparts dark grey merging into brown on lower abdomen; flanks, brown barred with dark grey; bill, black; legs, red.

Avicultural Notes   Tropical
    None recorded

Red-Billed Tree Partridge

Arborophila rubrisostris

Ref. 22.

(Salvadori 1879)

Sub-species
None recorded

Distribution
Sumatra, north and central.

Habitat
Mossy jungle gullies or dry brush covered hill ridges in mountainous areas.

Food
Seeds, vegetable matter, insects, beetles, etc.

Description
Adults. 10″ (25.4cm). Male. Head, throat and neck black with a few white spots on the sides of the crown and throat and a small

patch of the same colour on the chin; upperparts reddish olive-brown, barred with black; chest brown; upper breast and sides of the belly white with a large black spot on each feather; middle of belly white; flanks black barred with white. Female. Has rather more white on the lores and chin and is somewhat smaller; bill and feet, vermilion red; bare skin on face, crimson.

Avicultural Notes   Tropical
    None recorded

Red-Breasted Tree Partridge   *Arborophila hyperythra*
Ref. 23.   (Sharpe 1879)

    Sub-species
    A.h. hyperythra   - Sarawak up to N Borneo
    A.h. erythrophrys   - Mt Kinabalu

Distribution
    Northwest Borneo, north Borneo, Sarawak.
Habitat
    Secondary forest, river flats (rarely in trees), dense bamboo jungles.
Food
    Seeds, fruit, insects, acorns.
Description
    Adults. 11″ (28cm). Sexes alike. Upperparts olive-brown with black, a broad grey line from eye to nape; crown plain black with brown spots; chin and throat rufous; breast cinnamon; a broad band of black feathers with large white spots along sides of body from wing joints; abdomen white; skin around eye dark red, iris, grey; feet, salmon pink; bill, black.
Avicultural Notes   Tropical
    Recommended size of aviary Minimum size 6′ x 8′ (2m x 2.6m)
    Numbers in captivity   None recorded - 1978 and 1982 W.P.A. Census.

Egg colour	Pure white, glossy
Egg clutch size	8 - 10 eggs (wild)
Incubation period	Not known
Noise level	Can be loud according to reports from wild
Habits	A domed nest, will roost in low trees
Food	As Roulroul partridge
Novice selection	Not suitable

Hainan Hill Partridge
White-Eared Partridge
Ref. 24.
Sub-species
None recorded

Arborophila ardens
(Styan 1892)

Distribution
Endemic to Hainan Island. China.
Habitat
Forest areas.
Food
Seeds, berries, vegetable matter.
Description
Adults. 10" (25.4cm). Similar to *A. rufogularis*. Has some black barring on underparts; head mostly black with dark olive-brown crown, white eyebrow and ear coverts; throat black; neck streaked with black, rufous and white; lacks chestnut on flanks.
Avicultural Notes   **Temperate**
None recorded

Bamboo Partridge
Mountain Bamboo Partridge
Ref. 25.
Sub-species
B.f. fytchii

Bambusicola fytchii
(Gould 1863)

- W. China, Burma, N. Vietnam.

B.f. hopkinsoni   - Assam, S. Burma.

Distribution
Assam hills south of Brahmaputra River, Manipur, east Pakistan, west China, Burma, north Vietnam.

Habitat
Low elevations, found in open scrub jungle bordering pasture and rice fields and not predominantly restricted to bamboo forest as its name suggests.

Food
Berries, seed grain, various insects, buds and shoots.

Description
Adults. 14" (35.5cm). Sexes alike. A long-tailed rufous-brown partridge. Crown and nape rufous brown, face rufous-buff with a broad rufescent white supercilium to the nape, a broad dark rufous-brown or blackish line below and behind the eye; upper-parts grey-brown, broadly streaked with chestnut and spotted with blackish chestnut in scapulary region; vermiculated with grey-brown on lower back, rump and tail; wing quills chestnut brown, tail barred brown and buff; Chin, throat and foreneck rufous-buff; breast chestnut, spotted and streaked with white and grey; remainder of underparts buff, with large black heart- or moon-shaped spots, except on centre of abdomen and vent. Eyes, hazel or yellow-hazel; bill, dark horny brown; legs and feet, greenish-brown, claws, bluish, spurs, whitish horny.

Avicultural Notes	Temperate
Recommended size of aviary	Minimum size 6' x 6' (2m x 2m)
Numbers in captivity	8 - 1978, 24 - 1982, W.P.A. Census.
Egg colour	Creamy buff to deep warm buff, unspotted, fine textured and hard-shelled
Egg clutch size	4 - 6 eggs (wild)
Incubation period	18 - 19 days
Noise level	Fairly loud.
Habits	Mainly ground dwelling
Food	Pellets, mixed millets. Little

green food.

Novice selection   Not recommended

Chinese Bamboo Partridge
Ref. 26.

Bambusicola thoracica
(Temminck 1815)

Sub-species
B.t. thoracica   - China
B.t. sonorivox   - Taiwan

Distribution
China and Taiwan.

Habitat
Hills with jungle and tangle thickets. No preference to bamboo forests.

Food
Seed, grain, buds, shoots and berries.

Description
Adults. 10½" (26.7cm). Forehead to back of neck dusky grey, lighter from base of bill over eye to side of neck. Side of head below eye, throat and side of neck rufous, colour extending irregularly to upper back. Upperparts mottled deep ruddy and fulvous on slaty olive-grey. The feathers are undistinctive and finely marked darker. Primaries dusky, edged lighter; tertiaries tipped fulvous, lower back without mottlings. Tail deep rufous, finely barred with broken black. Breast from throat bluish-grey, colour extending to shoulders, bordered on barred lower side by rich ruddy-rufous; underparts yellowish-rufous, spotted with dark brown and ruddy; centre of belly unmarked; bill, and feet, dark brown.

Avicultural Notes   Temperate

Recommended size of aviary   Minimum size 6' x 6' (2m x 2m)
Numbers in captivity   69 - 1978, 120 - 1982,
      W.P.A. Census

Egg colour   Dark creamy to light brown
Egg clutch size   7 - 9 eggs (captive)

Incubation period	18 days
Noise level	Can be noisy in breeding season
Habits	Ground dwelling but will perch
Food	Pellets, mixed millets. Little green food.
Novice selection	Chicks can be difficult to rear, need live food to succeed.

Ferruginous Wood Partridge
Ref. 27.

Caloperdix oculea
(Temminck 1815)

Sub-species

C.o. oculea	- S. Thailand, Malaysia
C.o. sumatrana	- Sumatra
C.o. borneensis	- Borneo

Distribution
Thailand, Malaysia, Sumatra, Borneo.
Habitat
Montane forest, and dry sandy forest valley bottoms.
Food
Seeds, berries, grasses and beetles.
Description
Adults. 10½" (26.7cm). Sexes alike. Long-legged tree partridge. Rufous-buff head with dark chestnut crown and a black line behind the eye. Black lower hindneck, back and sides of body are with white to rufous-buff scales; upper belly and breast is unmarked, bright ferruginous. Rump and upper tail coverts black with light rufous 'v' shaped marks; tail, black; eyes, dark olive-brown; bill, black; feet, olive-green.

Avicultural Notes	Tropical
Recommended size of aviary	Min. size 6' x 8' (2m x 2.6m)
Numbers in captivity	4 - 1978, 13 - 1982, W.P.A. Census.
Egg colour	Pure white, glossy
Egg clutch size	8 - 10 eggs (wild)

Incubation period	18 - 20 days
Noise level	Reasonable
Habits	Ground dwelling
Food	Tropical partridge mixture, little fruit, few mealworms.
Novice selection	Not suitable
Special notes	This partridge builds a domed nest on the ground, having a hole at one side approx. 1″ off the ground.

Crimson-Headed Wood Partridge

Ref. 28.   *Haematortyx sanguiniceps*
(Sharpe 1879)

Sub-species
None known

Distribution
North Borneo.
Habitat
Mountain forest, prime forest with sandy valley bottoms.
Food
Berries and insects, together with small crustaceans.
Description
Adults. 10″ (25.4cm). Sexes different. Typical Wood Partridge. Male. General colour blackish-brown; crown and nape dull deep crimson; foreneck, chest and longer under tail coverts deep brilliant crimson; cheeks and throat paler crimson. Spurred legs in males, two and three recorded. Female. Has paler throat, more rufous, washed crimson and the face part of the neck and neck reddish-chestnut. Slightly smaller in size.

Avicultural Notes	Tropical
Recommended size of aviary	Min. size 6′ x 4′ (2m x 1.3m)
Numbers in captivity	Nil recorded 1978, W.P.A. Census.

Egg colour	Coffee-milk base with umber colour smeared in streaks
Egg clutch size	8 - 9 eggs (wild)
Incubation period	18 - 19 days
Noise level	Moderate
Habits	Ground dwelling
Food	Tropical partridge mixture, fruit, live food.
Novice selection	Not suitable
Special notes	Reputed to be difficult to maintain in captivity

Snow Partridge
Ref. 29.

Lerwa lerwa
(Hodgson 1833)

Sub-species
None recorded

Distribution
Afghanistan, Himalayas, western China.
Habitat
Hillside pastures, areas with fern and rhododendron bushes above 2,500m (8,000').
Food
Seeds, shoots, insects, greenfood.
Description
Adults. 15" (38.1cm). Sexes alike. Both closely barred black and white above, below largely deep chestnut, broadly streaked with whitish abdomen and flanks. Under tail coverts chestnut streaked with black and tipped with white. Legs and bill, bright red.

Avicultural Notes	Cold
Recommended size of aviary	Min. size 6' x 8' (2m x 2.6m)
Numbers in captivity	None recorded in 1978 W.P.A. Census.
Egg colour	Pale clear buff to dirty dark grey-

Tibetan Partridge

Himalayan Snowcock

Painting by H. Grönvold

Black Wood Partridge   Painting by H. Grönvold

Ferruginous Wood Partridge   Painting by Richard Robjent

	buff, blotched with reddish all over.
Egg clutch size	3 - 5 eggs (54.6 x 35.4 mm) (wild)
Incubation period	Not known
Noise level	Noisy, especially during the breeding season.
Habits	Ground dwelling
Food	Millets, pellets, few mealworms.
Novice selection	Not suitable.

Madagascar Partridge   *Margaroperdix madagascariensis*
Ref. 30.   (Scopoli 1786)

Distribution

Island of Madagascar, Réunion Is.

Habitat

Forest areas, heath areas of mountainous country.

Food

Berries, seed, roots, insects.

Description

Adults. 10″ (25.4cm). Male. Upperparts reddish-brown with shaft stripes of white and mostly with rufous or buff cross-bars; a line of black feathers with whitish shaft stripes down the middle of the head; sides of the head and throat black, with white stripes over the eye and along the sides of the throat; foreneck amd middle of chest chestnut; sides grey; middle of breast and belly black with oval white spots; sides and flanks mosltly chestnut; tail black barred with reddish-white; bill, black. Female. Black generally above, mixed with olive-brown with pale shaft stripes and bars as in the male; throat, sides of head and underparts mostly rufous-buff, the latter with concentric black lines on each feather; sides and flanks barred with black.

Avicultural Notes   Tropical

None recorded

Black Wood Partridge
Ref. 31.

Melanoperdix nigra
(Vigors 1829)

Sub-species
M.n. nigra — Malaysia, Sumatra.
M.n. borneensis — Borneo.

Distribution
Sumatra, Borneo, Malaysia.

Habitat
Dense forest, particularly in spiny stemless palm undergrowth. Lower montane forest.

Food
Seeds, roots, insects.

Description
Adults. 9½" (24.1cm). Sexes not alike. Male. Glossy black plumage diagnostic. Wings blackish brown. Bill, black. Female. Dark chestnut with the exception of a buffy white throat and belly; a few broad black bars on scapulars. Plain almost unmarked plumage. Bill, dark horn. Both sexes. Feet, pale blue, claws, pale horn.

Avicultural Notes	Tropical
Recommended size of aviary	Min. size 6' x 4' (2m x 1.3m)
Numbers in captivity	Nil recorded 1978, 15 - 1982. W.P.A. Census.
Egg colour	White with surface slightly rough and chalky
Egg clutch size	5 - 6 eggs (40 x 31.3mm)
Incubation period	18 - 19 days
Noise level	Reasonable
Habits	Mainly ground dwelling but will perch
Food	Tropical partridge mixture, little fruit, few mealworms.
Novice selection	Not suitable
Special notes	Subject to stress more than normal

Grey Partridge
Hungarian Partridge
Ref. 32.

Perdix perdix
(Linnaeus 1750)

Sub-species

P.p. perdix	- British Isles, W. & C. Europe
P.p. armoricana	- N.W. France
P.p. sphagnetorum	- N.E. Holland, N.W. Germany
P.p. hispaniensis	- Pyrenees, N. Spain
P.p. italica	- Italy
P.p. lucida	- N.E. Europe
P.p. robusta	- N.W. Russia
P.p. arenicola	- W.C. Russia
P.p. furvescens	- S.W. Russia, N. Iran
P.p. canescens	- Transcaucasia to N.W. Iran

Distribution
British Isles, central & eastern Europe, introduced to N. America, Australia, and New Zealand.

Habitat
Open country, farmland, moorland, downs and steppes, heaths, semi-desert, single tracts, and sand dunes.

Food
Seed, insects, greenfood.

Description
Adults. 12″ (30.5cm). Sexes alike. Male. Crown brown streaked with buff, remainder of head pale cinnamon, upperparts brown barred and striated with red-brown; striated with white or pale buff on wings; breast grey vermiculated with black and chestnut and with a distinctive inverted horseshoe mark on lower breast, chestnut; abdomen white, boldly barred with chestnut; tail with 18 feathers chestnut; eye has a red ring around the outside; bill, greenish-grey, legs and feet, slate-grey. Female. Similar with horseshoe mark usually smaller and sometimes white.

Avicultural Notes
Temperate

Recommended size of aviary   Minimum size 6′ x 6′ (2m x 2m)
Numbers in captivity   Bred in quantity for sport.
Egg colour   Olive brown

Egg clutch size	10 or more
Incubation period	25 days
Noise level	Low
Habits	Ground dwelling
Food	Pellets, mixed seed, greenfood
Novice selection	Not easy to rear until experienced, young need live food, if available, to start the eating use Starter crumbs.

Daurian Partridge
Bearded Partridge
Ref.33.

Perdix dauricae
(Pallas 1811)

Sub-species
P.d. dauricae	- E.C. Asia, Mongolia, N. China
P.d. castaneothorax	- S. Manchuria
P.d. turcomana	- E. Turkestan, E. Tien Shan
P.D. przewalski	- E. Namshans, N.W. China
P.d. suschkini	- C. Amur, Ussuriland

Distribution
Russia through to south Manchuria, north and west China, Mongolia and Turkestan.

Habitat
Mountain slopes and steppes with forest.

Food
Berries, various seeds, greenfood, insects.

Description
Adults. 10″ (24.5cm). Sexes similar. Male. Resembles the common partridge *(Perdix perdix)* but on chin it has a number of lanceolate feathers which form a beard. The horseshoe marking is black while the other colours are much paler. Female. Similar to those of European species.

Avicultural Notes   Cold
Recommended size of aviary   Minimum size 6′ x 6′ (2m x 2m)
Numbers in captivity   Nil recorded 1978 W.P.A. Census.

Egg colour	Olive-brown
Egg clutch size	10 eggs or more
Incubation period	26 days
Noise level	Low
Habits	Ground dwelling. Parents share rearing young.
Food	Pellets, mixed millets, greenfood
Novice selection	Rare in captivity.

Tibetan Partridge
Ladakh Partridge
Ref. 34.
  Sub-species
  P.h. hodgsoniae
  P.h. caraganae

Perdix hodgsoniae
(Hodgson 1857)

- Tibet, Nepal
- Ladakh

Distribution
Tibetan border to central Nepal and Sikkim.
Habitat
Rocky hillsides with scattered furze bushes, dwarf juniper and rhododendron scrub, grass and bush cover around crops. (Between 2,800 to 5,600 metres winter to summer.)
Food
Seeds, shoots, roots, possibly insects.
Description
Adults. 12″ (30.5cm). Sexes alike. A high altitude partridge. Head patterned with prominent white eyebrows running across chestnut forehead, chestnut ear coverts with a black cheekpatch. A dull chestnut collar at base and sides of hindneck. Upperparts buffy grey barred with blackish on upper back, vermiculated on lower back. Lateral tail feathers largely chestnut, underparts white, unmarked on chin and throat, barred with black on breast, more broadly with chestnut-brown on flanks, lower abdomen and under tail coverts, buff. Scapulars, tertiaries and wing coverts narrowly streaked and barred with buff. Iris, brown or red-brown, orbital skin deep velvety crimson in breeding season,

dull redddish crimson at other times. Bill, pale horny-green, legs and feet, pale greenish-brown.

Avicultural Notes	Cold
Recommended size of aviary	Minimum size 6' x 6' (2m x 2m)
Numbers in captivity	Nil in 1982, W.P.A. Census.
Egg colour	Dark brownish-buff, long, oval eggs, tinged with olive.
Egg clutch size	8 - 10 eggs (37.6 x 27.2mm)
Incubation period	24 - 26 days
Noise level	Reasonable
Habits	Generally ground dwelling
Food	Pellets, mixed millets, few mealworms.
Novice selection	Not suitable.
Special notes	Could prove difficult as this is a high altitude partridge. Builds a very small nest in the wild.

Stone Partridge
Ref. 35.

Ptilopachus petrosus
(Gmelin   )

Sub-species	
P.p. petrosus	- Gambia, Cameroun
P.p. saturator	- N.E. Cameroun
P.p. brehmi	- Lake Chad to Sudan
P.p. major	- N. Ethiopia
P.p. florentiae	- S. Sudan to N.E. Zaire, Uganda, Kenya

Distribution
Western, central and southern Sudan, Ethiopia, northeast Zaire and Kenya.

Habitat
Rocky hills and cliffs, also sandy scrub covered plains.

Food
Grass seeds and insects.

Description

Adults. 10″ (25.4cm). A small bird with a long thick tail, general colour blackish-brown mottled with brown and white, a clear buff patch on breast. Female has paler breast patch. Bill horn coloured, skin on face and feet red.

Avicultural Notes — **Temperate**

Recommended size of aviary	Minimum size 6′ x 6′ (2m x 2m)
Numbers in captivity	1 - 1978, nil in 1982, W.P.A. Census.
Egg colour	Pale stone or buff without gloss.
Egg clutch size	4 - 6 eggs (33 x 25mm)
Incubation period	Not known
Noise level	Can be loud, especially during the breeding season.
Habits	Prefers to run rather than fly.
Food	Mixed millets, small pellets, few mealworms.
Novice selection	Not suitable.

Long-Billed Wood Partridge

Ref. 36.

Rhizothera longirostris
(Temminck 1807)

Sub-species
R.l. longirostris   - Malaysia, Sumatra, W. Borneo
R.l. dulitensis   - N. Borneo

Distribution

Malaysia, Thailand, Sumatra, Borneo.

Habitat

Dry forest, especially bamboo up to 4,000′.
Note : *R.l. longirostris* - lowlands; *R.l. dulitensis* - montane.

Food

Berries, grasses, seeds and insects.

Description

Adults. 14″ (35.5cm). Sexes similar. Male. Grey collar around neck, upper breast and upper back and unmarked buff underparts diagnostic, nearly unmarked rusty brown head and throat with dark brown crown and nape and large, long distinctive strongly curved bill, lacks black and white scales on neck, back and sides as found in the Ferruginous Wood Partridge. Buffy grey rump, upper tail coverts and tail, legs yellowish and distinctive. Female. Similar, but grey of neck and breast replaced by rufous-chestnut, some buffy streaks on back; rump, upper tail coverts and tail tawny. Note : Nests in bamboo bushes, shallow scrape lined with root fibre and bamboo leaves.

Avicultural Notes	Tropical
Recommended size of aviary	Min. size 8' x 4' (2.6 x 1.3 m)
Numbers in captivity	Nil - 1978, and 1982, W.P.A. Census.
Egg colour	Long oval egg, ground colour very light, tinged with rose-red spots, smooth texture, somewhat glossy.
Egg clutch size	2 - 5 eggs
Incubation period	18 - 19 days
Noise level	Considered reasonable
Habits	Ground dwelling, but will alight in trees
Food	Tropical partridge mixture, fruit, live food.
Novice selection	Not recommended.

Crested Wood Partridge

Roulroul Partridge
Ref. 37.

Rollulus roulroul
(Scopoli 1786)

Sub-species
None known

Distribution

South Thailand, Malaysia, Sumatra, Borneo.

Habitat

Lowland forests, bamboo groves and clearings within old forest.

Food
Large fruits, seeds, various insects, including wood ants.

Description
Adults. 10″ (25.4cm) Sexes different. Typical Wood Partridge.
Male. Maroon crest, red orbital skin and patch on bill, white patch on crown; dark glossy plumage (appears black in poor light) reddish feet, wings dark brown. Eyes red; bill, upper mandible red; rest black. Female. Glossy green plumage with chestnut scapulars and rusty brown wings, dark grey head and reddish legs & orbital skin diagnostic. Eyes, red, bill, black, legs, red.

Avicultural Notes	Tropical
Recommended size of aviary	Min. size 6′ x 8′ (2m x 2.6m)
Numbers in captivity	306 - 1978, 576 - 1982, W.P.A. Census.
Egg colour	Dull yellowish-white eggs, pyriform shape.
Egg clutch size	8 - 10 eggs (39 x 32mm) (captive)
Incubation period	18 - 19 days
Noise level	A rather shrill plaintive whistle.
Habits	Normally ground dwelling but will perch.
Food	Tropical partridge mixture, a little fruit, a mealworm or two.
Novice selection	Not suitable
Special notes	Builds a domed nest with entrance hole approximately 1″ from the ground.

Caucasian Snowcock
Ref. 38.

Tetraogallus caucasicus
(March 1877)

Distribution
Caucasus Mountains.

Habitat
Higher ranges, mountainous areas.

Food
Young plant shoots and bulbous roots.
Description
Adults. 21″ (53.4cm). Sexes alike. Both male and female resembles *T. caspius* in general plumage, but the back of the head and nape are rust-red and there is a dull chocolate band down each side of the throat, the whole upper back is barred and mottled with black and buff and the chest is blackish grey irregularly barred and mottled with buff.
Avicultural Notes   Cold
None recorded

Caspian Snowcock   *Tetraogallus caspius*
Ref. 39.   (Gould 1853)

Sub-species
T.c. caspius   - Taurus Mts. to N. Iran
T.c. semenowtian schanskii   - Zagros Mts.(Iran)

Distribution
North Iran.
Habitat
Mountain slopes and hillsides.
Food
Roots, bulbs, vegetable matter.
Description
Adults. 24″ (71cm). Male. like *T. himalayensis*, but pale in general colour and easily distinguished by the grey chest, the absence of chestnut on the sides of the nape and head and by having the basal part of the inner flight feathers white. Female. Differs in having the grey feathers of the chest mottled with buff. Slightly smaller than male.
Avicultural Notes   Cold
None recorded.

Tibetan Snowcock
Ref. 40.

Tetraogallus tibetanus
(Gould 1853)

Sub-species	
T.t. tibetanus	- Parnia Mts.(W. Tibet)
T.t. tschimenensis	- N. Tibet
T.t. centralis	- W.E. & C. Tibet
T.t. przewalskii	- E. Tibet, W. Kansu
T.t. henrici	- W. China
T.t. aquilonifer	- S. Tibet, Sikkim

Distribution
Tibet, west China, Sikkim.

Habitat
Above the tree line, sparsely grass covered ridges. Snow patch covered alpine pastures.

Food
Vegetable matter, roots, tubers, berries and grasses.

Description
Adults. 20" (51cm). Sexes only differ slightly. Head and neck dark grey; sides of forehead, ear coverts and throat white. Back largely sandy grey and blackish grey, finely vermiculated and streaked with buff. Rump, upper tail coverts and central tail feathers rufous; rest of tail blackish brown with rufous tips; white wing patch; below largely white; throat and upper breast unmarked followed by a grey band separating them from rest of underparts which are broadly streaked with black, the streaks broadest on flanks and lower abdomen. Reddish legs.

Avicultural Notes	Cold
Recommended size of aviary	Min. size 12' x 8' (4 x 2.6m)
Numbers in captivity	Nil recorded, W.P.A. Census.
Egg colour	Pale yellowish-stone to rich reddish-buff with small blotches and specks of red-brown.
Egg clutch size	5 - 7 eggs (65.4 x 45.4mm)
Incubation period	27 - 28 days
Noise level	Particularly noisy during breeding season.

Habits	Ground dwelling
Food	Corn, pellets, green food.
Novice selection	Not suitable.
Special notes	Cock inclined to maul his hens in breeding season.

Altai Snowcock
Ref. 41.

Tetraogallus altaieus
(Grey 1842)

Sub-species	
T.a. altaicus	- Altai Mts., Sajan Mts.
T.a. orientalis	- N.W. Mongolia

Distribution
North western Mongolia, Altai Mountains.
Habitat
Mountainous areas.
Food
Roots, bulbous roots, vegetable matter.
Description
Adults. 23" (58.5 cm). Sexes alike. Male and female recognisable from *T. tibetanus* by having the sides of the neck grey and the basal part of the outer (primary) flight feathers white, but there is no white at the base of the secondaries. It may be distinguished from the other species by its white underparts and the feathers of the sides being uniformly white. Bill, blackish-horn colour, feet, orange-red. Female, slightly smaller.
Avicultural Notes   Cold
    None recorded.

Himalayan Snowcock
Ref. 42.

Tetraogallus himalayensis
(Gray 1842)

| Sub-species | |
| *T.h. sewerzowi* | - S.E. Turkestan |

T.h. himalayensis	- W. Himalayas, E. Afghanistan
T.h. bendi	- N.W. Afghanistan
T.h. grombczewskii	- W. Kwenlum Mts.
T.h. koslowi	- Humboldt & S. Kokonor Mts.

Distribution
Turkestan, Himalayas, and Afghanistan.

Habitat
Steep alpine pastures near snowline, bare stony ridges above tree line.

Food
Bulbous roots and tubers, green vegetable matter.

Description
Adults. 28″ (72cm). Largely grey, white, chestnut and black streaked and vermiculated plumage. White throat separated by a broken chestnut collar from dark grey underparts and white under tail coverts are diagnostic. Yellow eye stripe during breeding season.

Avicultural Notes

	Cold
Recommended size of aviary	Large aviary. Minimum size 24′ x 12′ (8m x 4m)
Numbers in captivity	Nil - 1978, 60 in 1982, W.P.A. Census.
Egg colour	Pale yellow-stone to rich reddish -buff with specks of red-brown.
Egg clutch size	5 - 7 eggs
Incubation period	27 - 28 days
Noise level	Noisy during breeding season.
Habits	Mainly ground dwelling
Food	Pellets, grain, greenfood.
Novice selection	Rare, not suitable.

Verreaux's Monal Partridge
Ref. 43.

Tetraophasis obscurus
(Verreaux 1869)

Distribution
Northeast Tibet, west China.

Habitat
Bush covered rocks and ravines in a wooded area.
Food
Bulbous roots, plant shoots.
Description
Adults. 18.6" (47.4cm). Sexes alike. Both sexes are mostly dull olive-brown, barred with buff on the wings, below spotted grey with black shading into buff on the belly. Distinguished by having the chin, throat and forepart of the neck dark chestnut. Female smaller.
Avicultural Notes   Cold
None recorded

Szechenyi's Monal Partridge   *Tetraophasis szechenyii*
Pheasant Grouse   (Madarasz 1885)
Ref. 44.
Distribution
East Tibet, southwest China, provinces of Szechuan, Yunnan.
Habitat
Fir forest and rhododendron scrub areas near rocky ravines at altitudes between 3,350 and 4,6000 metres (10,800' and 15,000').
Food
Bulbous roots and green vegetation.
Description
Adults. 25" (64cm). Sexes alike. A large pheasant type bird, plain coloured, brownish grey narrowly streaked with black crown, dark brown hindneck and upper back, lower back and rump grey, feathers growing darker at edges. Throat and chin rust to fawn, upper breast dark grey, underparts browner-grey. As with lower back and rump the underparts feathers are edged with rust, together with rusty and chestnut spots, outer tail feathers with black and white tips.
Avicultural Notes   Cold
None recorded

Chestnut-breasted Tree Partridge *Tropicoperdix charltonii*
Scaly-Breasted Partridge   (Eyton 1845)
Ref. 45.

Sub-species
T.c. charltonii   - S Thailand, Malaysia
T.c. atjehensis   - N Sumatra
T.c. tonkinensis   - N Vietnam
T.c. graydoni   - Borneo

Distribution
Thailand, Malaysia, Sumatra, Vietnam, Borneo.

Habitat
Hill jungle, prefers drier types.

Food
Seeds, insects, berries.

Description
Adults. 11″ (28cm). Sexes alike. Crown brown, forehead streaked above the eye and nape, black speckled with white; orange skin around the eye; chestnut patch above the eye, rest of upperparts including wing and tail, brown vermiculated with buff and darker brown; chin and throat white speckled with black; side of neck and band around base of throat black. Upper breast rich chestnut; lower breast and flanks barred buff and black; rest of upperparts buff, merging into whitish on the abdomen. Bill, blackish, red, at base; legs, yellowish.

Avicultural Notes   **Temperate**
None recorded

Green-Legged Hill Partridge   *Tropicoperdix chloropus*
Ref. 46.   (Blyth 1859)

Sub-species
T.c. chloropus   - N. Burma to W. & S. Thailand
T.c. olivacea   - Laos, Cambodia
T.c. cognacqi   - S. Vietnam

Distribution
Northern South Vietnam, north Burma, Thailand, Laos, Cambodia.
Habitat
Frequent forests and thickets at low altitudes.
Food
Insects, seeds, vegetable matter.
Description
Adults. 12″ (30.5cm). Sexes alike. Upper parts olive-brown; throat has black spots, complete bright ferruginous collar with black spots; broad olive band across upper breast; remaining underparts bright ferruginous, much paler on belly and marked with black on sides and under tail coverts. Juveniles have upperparts and wings dark reddish-brown, narrowly barred everywhere with black except on the head; throat and neck pale brown; breast band and sides of body reddish-brown; upper belly pale buff with broad black streaks; remaining underparts whitish.
Avicultural Notes
None recorded

Temperate

Annamese Hill Partridge
Ref. 47.

Tropicoperdix merlini
(   )

Sub-species
T.m. merlini   - C. Vietnam
T.m. vivida   - E.C. Vietnam

Distribution
Central and eastern Vietnam.
Habitat
Forested areas, mountainous regions.
Food
Seeds, berries and insects.

Description

Adults. 10″ (25.4cm). Sexes alike. Crown dark brown, forehead above and below the eye white, speckled with black, merging into chestnut around the throat, upperparts including wings and tail mottled chocolate brown, chin and upper throat speckled white, breast chestnut flecked with black, lower breast chestnut merging into white, rump chocolate brown, bill, horn-colour, legs, yellowish.

Avicultural Notes   Temperate

None recorded.

Note:

The birds shown as being held in captivity recorded in the W.P.A. Census does not infer that all the specimens held in captivity have been recorded.

CHAPTER 6

BREEDING REQUIREMENTS

Environment

The housing should be adequate for the specie of Partridge to be kept and a guide to their respective minimum requirement is detailed in Chapter 5. Protection from extremes of temperature and rainfall are all important, as is access to clean water at all times. Should pens become very muddy, this will in turn cause a build-up of disease. Light and temperature stimulates breeding condition, but it is not synchronised in the male and the female. Over the years I have considered the possibility of force breeding rare birds, so as to obtain the maximum number in a season, but conclude that it is far better to obtain a few good and healthy chicks, rather than a lot of weaklings which will become degenerate stock in the future.

In-Breeding

Birds tend to be weaker, lack vigour, and hence poor display. The cocks produce only small quantities of inferior sperm. Also it can be the fault of either the hen or the cock when the germ dies before development, giving every appearance of an infertile egg. New blood or breeding to another strain has the opposite effect; it gives vigour, for as each bird has its recessive traits, so the dominant aspects of both parent birds appear in their young.

Health

Internal parasites, such as the gape and threadworms, are a common cause of poor production, and while the birds may appear to be in good condition, could well have some underlying disease which makes them unproductive or even infertile. Worms will upset a birds nutrition therefore all your birds should be wormed regularly. Avian tuberculosis, aspergillosis and coccidiosis are common infections where birds are kept on the same ground for many years. Birds with deformed feet can give problems and prevent a successful mating. A watch must be kept for signs of external parasites, fleas, lice, mites, etc., as they can become a constant irritation and affect the health of your birds. There are many suitable brands of insecticide available on the market today. Your birds should be treated before each breeding season.

Stress

Pen management and bad environment is one of the main causes of stress. Pens which are too small or have poor light can again give poor results. Partridge which spend their time running up and down the wire of their pens cannot be expected to give fertile eggs. The presence of potential predators, such as cats, dogs, and children will not allow your birds to settle and produce good results. Another aspect is bullying by fellow birds. It is always preferable to house only one pair of each species and have suitable solid partitions between pairs, as the male bird will constantly run up and down the wire trying to fight with his next door neighbour, then mating with his hen bird to show dominance. In general Partridge are monogamous and will only mate with one hen, leaving the remaining hens infertile; the only exception is the traditional gamebird which has been bred over the years on an intensive basis; the Grey, Red-Legged, and Chukar fall into this group.

Nutrition

Inadequate and poor food can affect fertility and in extreme cases the hen birds just do not lay eggs, and those which do could well be infertile. The same applies to the cock birds which are unable to fertilise them. Therefore a balanced diet is most important if success is to be achieved.

Fertility

As a general rule, Partridge are good for four to seven years, but the age of the male has a major influence on fertility and the resultant young stock. Although your birds may show that they are sexually mature, it does not mean you will automatically obtain the results you expect; good husbandry is all important. Partridge can be classed as an exotic species, and therefore most breeders continue to set eggs even when their birds are old, whereas breeding stock of gamebird species are usually released before fertility has fallen to a low level.

Stock

The age of the parents has a marked influence on hatchability. Eggs from very young birds (especially late hatch) will usually give a poor hatch rate from either weak germs or immaturity. Most Partridge are often sexually mature in their first year, but one does not normally obtain good results until a second year in many species.

Housing

The birds must be housed in an area suitable for each species, taking into account such features as its natural habitat, time of year, weather conditions, temperature, and the amount of light available. Birds must be clean and above all, contented.

Conditions

As already stressed, one cannot expect to obtain good breeding results if your stock is housed in cold, draughty pens, with no shelter from the elements. Even in the wild you will see gamebirds sheltering against high winds and heavy rain; therefore your captive stock will expect to be able to do the same.

Laying Season

If your birds are housed outside throughout the year, most species will start to lay in late April or early May, being stimulated by the warmer weather and longer days. They will continue until late July or mid August, again this is dependent on the weather. If your birds are housed inside, it is most likely they will show signs of breeding, and start laying, much earlier in the year. The amount of light available during the day, plus its length, is all important for your birds to come into condition. However, it is not recommended to force your birds into condition, due to the possibility of obtaining poor stock — allow the natural seasons to take their course. Needless to say the reverse also rules; reduced amount of light can overcome the stimulation with resultant detriment to the egg. indeed, no eggs at all.

Egg Eating

Should you find egg eating becoming a problem, use an old country method to overcome this. Take an egg similar to the birds' own, blow out the contents and fill with ordinary household mustard. Place the egg where the birds would normally lay. The birds will soon find it, and quickly go off the idea. Alternatively, obtain a china or wooden egg of a similar size and shape, place in the nest, and the birds will soon lose interest in trying to break into the egg.

Temperature

Variations in temperature will soon affect egg production; as with inadequate light, the effect may not be enough to reduce the number of eggs laid, but could well affect the hatchability.

Natural Food

Food compounders do try extremely hard to produce a diet similar to that in the wild, and include all the elements possible to produce strong and healthy birds. However, it is an undoubted fact that birds housed in an area where there is natural food such as berries, seeds and insects, increase the hatchability of their eggs. Unfortunately, most breeders cannot afford to have large planted pens for one pair of Partridge, apart from the parasitic infection which Partridge are likely to acquire. So, to keep ones birds on sand or wire floors will eliminate the problems of infection while a good formulated food, together with a constant supply of clean water, will help in giving extremely good results. They will enjoy clean berries or greenfood collected and given in season.

Keeping Records

It is always useful to record the number of eggs laid by each pair of birds and the results obtained. This will enable you to see which birds are giving a good hatch rate, and those which are not and require attention. As a routine, mark each egg laid with the date and a code for each pair of a certain species, as it will enable you to keep track of the eggs during incubation. Use one of those markers now available to mark packets of food destined for the freezer; these are usually non-toxic and unaffected by damp. Also record the same information in a book against each breeding pair. When marking the eggs, remember, not to press too hard — eggs are fragile.

Storage of Eggs

All eggs are best stored at about 55°F. (12.7°C.). Fluctuation in temperature can be very damaging, and give poor results.

Partridge normally lay large clutches of eggs in the wild and have no trouble in storing them. The first eggs laid can often be well over three weeks of age before the hen will start to sit, yet hatch just as well as the last egg laid. The same eggs correctly stored and then placed in an incubator should achieve a similar hatch rate. If the same eggs are given to a bantam the hatch is normally the same as with the parent bird. There is some evidence that if eggs which are to be stored for some length of time are warmed to 80°F. (26.6°C.) for a few minutes each day, combined with turning, the hatch rate will improve. (This is not recommended to be undertaken by the novice.)

This is in fact what the mother bird does to her own eggs during the time she is waiting to make up a complete clutch, also she rubs natural preen gland oils from her feathers on them, which helps to clean the eggs and gives them a covering of lysozyme, which acts as a barrier against infection. This is one point in favour of using a broody over an incubator. Growth within an egg will commence if stored at a temperature above 70°F. (21.1°C.); this growth will be very slow and weak. If prolonged, the embryo will either die or be so weak that it will not survive major growth later in its development. Prolonged periods of cold will also cause the embryo to die. The size of the air cell can be used to establish the quality of an egg. Large air cells usually denote eggs which have been badly stored.

Egg Storage Humidity

With a storage temperature of 55°F. (12.7°C.) the humidity needs to be between 75% and 85%. Too low can mean evaporation of the egg contents, and too high will cause water to condense on the shell, allowing bacteria and moulds to penetrate, thus destroying the embryo.

Storage Time

For the best results always try to set all eggs as soon as possible after they are laid, and do not wait until the full clutch is complete.

Ideally, eggs should not be kept for more than a week; if stored for longer periods they tend to produce smaller chicks and will take longer to hatch. This is where an incubator has an advantage, as eggs can be set once they are cooled after laying, provided you have adequate rearing facilities for small numbers of chicks when they hatch.

Turning of Eggs

Eggs held in storage should be turned at least twice a day. The reason for this is that the yolk tends to float to the highest part of the egg, and if left in contact with one part of the shell for any length of time it can stick, thus upsetting development. Eggs are best stored either on their side or large end up.

Damaged Eggs

Should an egg be cracked and too valuable to discard, providing

Reliable Vision Incubator

Reliable Thermostat Co Ltd, Bramley, Rotherham, Yorkshire.

the cracks are not too large, it can be painted with nail varnish to prevent excess evaporation and bacteria entering. One must be prepared to hatch a malformed chick if care is not taken.

Candling of Eggs

Infertile eggs can seriously affect the chances of hatching the remaining eggs, therefore all your eggs should be candled between four and seven days; that is to say — the egg is placed over a bright light, preferably housed in a box with a ½" (12.5 mm) hole in the top, over which the egg is placed, for a very short time. The light will illuminate the contents of the shell showing the embryo as a black dot, surrounded by small blood vessels.

Daily Changes in the Weight and the Form of the Developing Chick Embryo
(Adapted from Romanoff)

1 DAY (0.0002 GRAM)	2 DAYS (0.003 GRAM)	3 DAYS (0.02 GRAM)	4 DAYS (0.05 GRAM)	5 DAYS (0.13 GRAM)	6 DAYS (0.29 GRAM)	7 DAYS (0.57 GRAM)
8 DAYS (1.15 GRAMS)	9 DAYS (1.53 GRAMS)	10 DAYS (2.26 GRAMS)	11 DAYS (3.68 GRAMS)	12 DAYS (5.07 GRAMS)	13 DAYS (7.37 GRAMS)	14 DAYS (9.74 GRAMS)
15 DAYS (12.00 GRAMS)	16 DAYS (15.98 GRAMS)	17 DAYS (18.59 GRAMS)	18 DAYS (21.83 GRAMS)	19 DAYS (25.62 GRAMS)	20 DAYS (30.21 GRAMS)	21 DAYS (HATCHED)

Always, if in doubt, leave the egg to incubate for a little longer. Should the egg be completely clear, remove, say after 14 days. The humidity level of the egg can be seen from the egg's air space; if it is very small after the first weel, humidity must be reduced, on the other hand, if too large (say a third of the egg), it must be increased.

Hatching by Parents

Using the parent bird is by far the best method of hatching eggs. The hen's natural ability far outweighs any mechanised devices, being able to turn the eggs when required, having them kept at the correct temperature, and moisture, to finally hatching them. There are certain pitfalls, such as whether the hen bird will be able to sit undisturbed for the period of incubation, the siting of the nest away from direct sunlight, and finally, whether the pen in which she has nested is secure against the young escaping through the wire, or conversely, vermin entering; both can be a hazard to the chicks. If is is at all possible this method of breeding Partridge must be encouraged, as the progeny will be much stronger than those artificially bred. Also they retain the instinct to breed naturally, which is so important when holding captive stock, for eventual re-introduction back to the wild.

Hatching using a Bantam

Before the modern electric incubator became popular, the broody bantam was the traditional way of rearing gamebirds. This method, as with hatching by the parent bird, has its merits, as it is the nearest way of producing chicks naturally. Selection of the bantam is most important; in general she should be small and compact, to accommodate the smaller species of chick when first hatched, and should you contemplate placing valuable eggs or chicks under her, you must at least have some knowledge of how she has performed in previous years. It is not unknown for a broody to decide to stand up on her eggs, and allow them to become cold for no real reason. She can also become restless due to lice or fleas, and tread on her eggs, breaking them in the process. Before actually giving her the eggs to incubate, it is always wise to test whether she is going to sit tight, therefore place some dummy eggs under her for a few days to be quite sure, before committing the more valuable eggs.

Sitting Box

For a broody to successfully hatch her eggs, she must have peace and quiet. If she is placed in darkness, or limited light to sit, this will improve her steadiness during incubation. A box measuring 12″ (304mm) square inside measurement and approximately the same height should be quite adequate for one small broody. If the box is

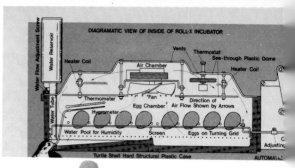

DIAGRAMATIC VIEW OF INSIDE OF ROLL-X INCUBATOR

The ROLL-X INCUBATOR

by

Marsh

RXIA

TX5A

TX5M

Turn-X Incubators

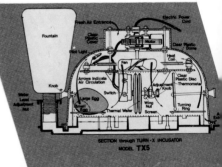

SECTION through TURN-X INCUBATOR
MODEL TX5

too large, she will probably move around and let the eggs roll away from her and get chilled. The reverse if too small — she will be too cramped and uncomfortable, which will make her restless. The front of the box can have a door which closes down, or a piece of sacking which is secured at the top, and held in place at the bottom by two bricks. The box must, of course, have some ventilation, a row of ½" (12.5mm) holes around the top of the box will be quite satisfactory.

Incubators

During the last few years, there have been major advances in the design and understanding of small incubators. The latest electrically powered models use a solid-state temperature control unit rather than the old capsule which operated the microswitch to control the temperature and the variations this incurred. The early incubators were heated by use of paraffin; the machine having a traditional oil heater attached to its side, which has a metal chimney with two outlets, one at the top and the other on the side entering the top of the egg chamber of the incubator; a capsule within the egg chamber regulates the flow of hot air from the heater. The requirements of the average breeder can be quite adequately catered for by one of the small electrically operated machines currently available, which have a single layer capacity up to 240 eggs at one time. Should you own one of these older models, it is well worth keeping the operating instructions, as they do need adjustment from time to time.

There are two basic types of electrically operated incubator available. The still air, or convection type, and the moving air incubator. The first type has a heater element in the top of the machine, and as the heated air cools, it passes around the eggs and through the air vents at the sides of the machine just below the heater elements. In the case of the moving air type, it is similar in construction but has a small fan to circulate the air around the eggs. The fan and heater in this type are usually controlled by a microswitch operated by a capsule, similar to those used in the paraffin incubator. With the solid-state control, the temperature is no longer controlled by the rise and fall of the capsule via several levers to transmit the result, but by an electrical component which senses variations of temperature within itself and in turn operates a switch to the heater, thus giving much greater accuracy.

My own success over the years has been achieved by using a small still air machine with the eggs being hand turned twice a day. This means turning each egg through 180° every time, and reversing the tray so that those eggs in the front return to the rear, and those on the right face to the left. This ensures that all the eggs receive equal heat. Before returning to the incubator, they should be sprayed with luke warm water, depending on the humidity required.

Of course, there are also machines available which will turn your eggs automatically, thus eliminating the time spent on what can be a very boring job. In addition, there is a trend for manufacturers to produce machines with clear tops or covers, so that the eggs can be viewed at all times.

Humidity Control

There are usually water trays placed in the bottom of most incubators today which require topping up with water to maintain the required humidity. Later models have a drip feed water supply system into the trays. Check by candling the eggs.

Temperatures for Partridge

Depending on the type of incubator, one wants to achieve a temperature around 101° - 102°F. (38.8°C.) on the upper surfaces of the eggs. I suggest you note the makers instructions to obtain the same result. My own still air incubators run at this temperature. (For game partridge set still-air incubators at 103.5°F. 2″ above the floor of the egg tray, or 99.7°F for moving-air incubators.)

Siting of the Incubator

Best results can be obtained when the incubator is positioned out of the direct sunlight and in a room where the temperature does not vary much from 60°F. (15.5°C.). There must be good ventilation as air flow is an important factor when using an incubator, but no draught. Humidity is also a factor to be considered, the optimum relative humidity should be around 50% - 60% (wetbulb reading = 86° - 89°F.). Incubators with a high air flow rate need to be humid, therefore if it is at all possible, site your incubator in an old outhouse or stable where the temperature does not fluctuate. The walls, if made of stone or brick, will hold a certain amount of moisture which will help with humidity. It is well worth selecting the right spot.

High Temperature in Incubator

Always adjust your incubator well before setting the eggs; if the temperature remains higher than required it could cause a nil hatch, but if only for a limited time, it can result in some dead in shell. Unfortunately the damage cannot be repaired, therefore careful adjustment prior to incubation is all important.

Egg incubated with to high humidity. Air bubble too small. Chick will pip below the bubble and strangle on fluid.

Egg incubated with low humidity. Air bubble too large. Fluids have dried up. Chick will be weak and become stuck to the shell when it pips.

Egg incubated with correct humidity. Air bubble is the right size. Chick will pip above the dotted line and remove the bubble as a door.

Egg with little end up. Chick will be disoriented. Will pip at wrong end and drown in the fluids.

Low Temperature in Incubator

This acts in reverse to high temperatures, depending on how low, and reflects a degree of delay in hatching taking place. It does not usually increase mortality, but the continual opening of the incubator — thus lowering the temperature — will give poor results; the same with candling the eggs too often, allowing the incubator to cool.

The Incubator as a Hatcher

Having completed the required incubation period, the chicks will usually hatch; in the case of partridge the clutch of eggs will all hatch within a few hours of each other. This will mean that the early chicks will be running between the remaining eggs in the incubator, so some people advise removing the eggs prior to hatching and placing them in a second incubator to act as a hatcher, to allow the chicks to dry off. A chick does not need to eat for at least 12 - 24 hours as it will digest and survive on its yolk sac, but should be feeding and drinking properly at least 48 hours after hatching.

Brooders

When your chicks are completely dry and downy they can be placed in a brooder box as illustrated. This is a box with an open top covered with small mesh wire netting, and an electric light bulb mounted on an adjustable base at the rear. You will see that there are two bulbs to each compartment, as a safeguard in the case of one fusing. Normally, the season starts with two 60 watt red or blue bulbs to obtain the required temperature of 95°F. (35°C.). As the ambient temperature rises during the season, one of the bulbs is removed and replaced by a 5 - 8 watt nite-light, so that light is still available, at the same time reducing heat. A recent idea to be successfully used is wiring into the bulbs' electrical circuit a light dimmer as used in the home; although rather expensive initially, one can regulate the heat required.

Floor Covering

There are a number of floor coverings which can be used. I favour the use of corrugated paper for two reasons. Firstly, the chicks can gain a secure foothold on the corrugations, and secondly, food can be sprinkled over the floor in front of the chicks, and is not scattered into the corners, as with flat surfaces. Other people use rolled oats very successfully, which gives the chicks something to peck at as well as a good foothold.

Food and Water

For the smaller species of partridge you must ensure that the food is ground small enough, and that the water trough is not too large, to prevent the chicks from drowning. The plastic fountain used for cage birds is ideal in the early days.

Starter Foods

As already mentioned in Chapter 4, there are specially for-mulated foods available as starter crumbs which are quite adequate for the majority of species, and it is always best, at least for the more difficult species, to have the compounded diet as a base food. One of the ways to get your day old chicks to start eating is to sprinkle a little on their backs. This causes interest and starts them pecking. In the case of the tropical species or those which need an insectile diet, get-ting them started can prove difficult; in the wild the parent birds will pick up an insect and offer it to the chick, therefore in the early days of its life it is more inclined to look up for its food than to look on the floor. There are two ways to overcome this problem; the first is to break a mealworm in half and offer the broken end to the chick on the end of a pair of tweezers; it is normally interested and takes the worm. One worm every two to four hours will keep the bird alive. Also sprinkle on the floor a mixture of 1:1 ground chick starter crumbs and fine insectile food. The chick will become interested in the food at its feet and begin to peck at it. The second way is to hatch a Coturnix Quail chick alongside the partridge you wish to rear and have it running with them; you may still have to feed mealworms but the quail will soon start scratching in the mixture and encourage the partridge chicks to do the same. Other food items can also be added, such as hardboiled egg pressed through a grinder giving eggworms, a little chopped lettuce or grated cheese. Clean water and a little fine grit must always be available. Some people like to add an antibiotic to the drinking water to minimise the effects of stress, but I prefer not to, as when the bird does have to be given an antibiotic the effect is reduced, but like many things when rearing birds, one always has likes and dislikes. When the chicks are about two weeks old, start to introduce some larger size of food; at six weeks your chicks can well start to have the adult mixture introduced.

Brooding Temperature

At day-old stage, the temperature should be around 95°F. (35°C.), this being reduced to about 85°F. (29°C.) by two weeks, when the chicks can be transferred to a larger brooder until they are fully feathered, heat being required only at nights. This is usually around 5 - 6 weeks depending on the species.

Alternative Types of Brooder Heating

Some breeders prefer to use a black heat lamp of 150 watts which is hung over the chicks to give the required heat. The height from the ground for the correct temperature will be determined by trial and error — the chicks will huddle together if they are cold, so lower the lamp; if they are too hot they will spread out, and the lamp needs to be raised. When black heat is used some form of additional light is required, if natural light is not available. Caution — When using this type of heater always check that it is working when you switch on, since no light is emittted from it.

Transfer to the Outside

Only when your chicks have become fully fledged, and off heat, should you consider placing them out of doors. It is as well to treat your young stock in the same way as adults at this stage, bearing in

5′ × 5′ Brooder House with floor

10′ × 6′ Shelter Pen—for rearing partridge

Farm Equipment and Supply Company,
Tumby, Boston, Lincolnshire.

c/o Lincolnshire Pheasantries
Mareham-le-Fen (065-83) 218

mind they will need a dry and draught proof shelter to roost in at night.

Bantam Rearing of Partridge

Once the chicks have hatched and are dry, they should have a small run attached to the coop, so that the chicks can have room to move around. A diet of ground starter chick crumbs can be given, with a supply of clean water and grit, the hen being fed mixed corn twice a day. In the case of the more difficult species being reared by a small bantam: There is some merit in this method as the hen will help the chicks to find food in the early days, but there are certain pitfalls — bantams can carry disease, or may stand on a rare chick. Assuming you decide to use a bantam, the diet for the chicks will be the same as if you were rearing in a brooder box. As the food offered is expensive, it is well worth containing the hen behind bars in her coop, allowing the chicks to run to the food placed within the hen's reach, but not allowing her to scratch and scatter it across the ground. Waste food will soon go bad, and can cause problems. A broody will take care of her chicks very well up to the stage when they are fully fledged, brooding them as and when required. They can be moved when independent of their mother.

CHAPTER 7

PARTRIDGE FOR THE SMALL SHOOTING ESTATE

This chapter is designed to give the person with a small estate, or a farm which has land suitable to hold game for shooting purposes, some guidance in holding the stock, and raising additional birds to maintain a healthy population. Some landowners and farmers are keen on their shooting and will give their game every consideration. They will cut their precious hay only when their even more precious partridges have hatched safely and left the field, also they will not use any poisonous insecticides on the pea crops because these chemicals might kill the gamebirds. On the other hand, there are also farmers and landowners who will pull up every hedge and bush to cultivate every square inch of soil until they have a highly efficient food factory, neatly boxed in with barbed wire. Under this type of management the game simply has to take its chance with farm machines and chemicals — although the farmer nevertheless often expects some sport.

Partridge as a Game Crop

In many areas where natural conditions for the increase of wild game are potentially good, the rearing of birds may be unnecessary. Instead it will be important to maintain the right habitat, improving it wherever possible. The birds' food supply, particularly in winter, is often a key factor, and some control of their natural enemies may be necessary at certain seasons. In the uplands of hot countries lack of water may be a problem, however game may simply need initial encouragement. Reared birds of a wild or hardy strain can be planted out as seed stock and if properly looked after will, in due course, establish themselves. Most conservation work will fit in with the daily routine on the farm. A modest shoot will only take the equivalent labour involved in maintaining a normal garden.

Habitat

The barbed wire fence has had the greatest impact on farm wildlife. The wire fence replaces the warm friendly hedgerows and it is the most obvious alteration to gamebird habitat in the countryside. It should be realised by everyone interested in shooting that the foundation stone on which all management is based is habitat; fields, woods, hedges, and open ground are the natural range of the important British game species — particularly the pheasant, which moves from cover into the open and back again. The Grey and Redlegged Partridges are normally seen out on fields or grassland but need a proportion of taller cover if they are to survive and breed successfully. In the UK hedgerows have looked after their needs for centuries, but the modern trend towards intensive farming have deprived them of even a minimum of nesting sites in some parts of the country. This factor may not seem vital to the layman, but it has been demonstrated with the Bobwhite Quail in America that when the total hedgerow falls below a certain figure per square mile the breeding population vanishes completely. The birds do not, as we might expect, hang on until the last pair inhabits the last stretch of hedge. It has been found that in Norfolk, England, hedges together with a grassy bank of about 7 ft. (2.3m) are quite sufficient for Partridges to nest. Of course, hedges are not the only source of cover. Between the wars in Hungary, an area famous for partridges, there were few hedgerows, but other cover was available, in particular strip cultivation by the peasant farmers. Partridges will thrive wherever there are areas of rough, ungrazed grass to give secure nest sites and shelter. Major nest losses among Partridges occur when a proportion of hedgerow is removed, and the hen birds are forced to resort to insecure sites in the open. Under these conditions many eggs and chicks will be lost to predators.

Vermin Control

It is a normal thing for us to control weeds, insects, rodents and other pests in order to harvest better crops; the same applies to Partridge to obtain the best breeding and stocking results. In areas of the world where the public are allowed to shoot off vast areas of land, intense vermin control is not required, but in areas where a high density of game is encouraged for private shooting purposes, the selective control of the gamebirds' worst enemies will be of great importance. A positive way of controlling predators is not only by shooting, but by trapping, using a humane spring trap, such as the Mk II Fenn or Sawyer trap. The smaller mammalian predators such as rats, stoats, weasels, hedgehogs and mink, can be controlled by a network of tunnel traps strategically sited throughout the area of habitat. Tunnel traps are simply small traps set in natural or artificial tunnels, attractively situated in the normal thoroughfare of these mammals. The tunnels should be approximately 2ft (0.6m) long, large enough to house a trap and allowing it to operate freely. They are set unbaited as most ground predators are curious enough to hunt into most holes. All traps should be examined daily and re-set frequently, whether they have been sprung or not. Working parts may well get blocked with mud and leaves. The continental box trap is an alternative, again not baited, and sited in the normal runs of the predators. The fox is possibly the only major large predator in the UK; normally your local hunt of foxhounds will assist in the removal of foxes, but in those areas where they do not exist you must resort to either shooting, snaring, or gassing in their earth. It must be left to the individual to decide the best method to adopt.

Rooks and crows are usually controlled by shooting, and magpies and jays must never be allowed to breed on the farm or estate where dense population of Partridge is required. Hawks and falcons should not be killed, most are protected by law.

Winter Management

Food and shelter is obtained by the provision of suitable cover; crop planning is particularly important and patches of stubble in the form of undersown leys are most valuable when dotted about all over the shoot. Winter cereals too are obviously very useful, together with grass break crops. Only in this way can breeding stock be held, to give good production when the hatching years — with a warm dry June — come along.

Hand feeding of Partridges is now a thing of the past due to the time it consumes; the hopper has now taken its place. Feeding points can be near ricks or in the lee of shelter-belts or hedges, in pits or uncultivated field corners. The Grey Partridge is not inclined to stray far, so hoppers are highly suitable for this species. You can simply make your hoppers from empty oil drums or other suitable containers. Cut four vertical slits some 3" (7.8cm) long, near the bottom of the drum, wide enough for the grain to fall out when pecked or tapped by the Partridge. In the first place the drum can be placed on the ground surrounded by straw with grain on the ground near each slot. Continue placing grain at these points until the birds start to use the hopper, then the drum can be lifted off the ground onto two bricks (one brick high). Ensure that the bricks do not project from under the hopper allowing sparrows or rats to reach the grain. Once the birds are used to this method of feeding the height can be increased to two bricks height from the ground. To assist in holding your gamebirds the Farmer/Sportsman can find a few odd corners to sow some food patches to give sunflower, maize, canary seed, buckwheat, caraway, sweet clover, marrowstem kale and mida rape (a mixture recommended by the Game Conservancy). Corn sown in early May.

Types of Partridge suitable for the small estate

1) The English Grey or Hungarian Partridge   *Perdix perdix*
2) The Red-Legged or French Partridge   *Alectorus rufa*
3) The Chukar Partridge   *Alectorus chukar*
4) The Ogridge (a hybrid between the Chukar and Red-Legged).

The Grey Partridge is the endemic species to the UK and is found in most parts of the country, although since the sixties it has reduced in numbers. This species is popular with most shoots, but has the tendency to pack into large numbers and fly over one gun, therefore their release must be carefully controlled. The Red-Legged Partridge being an introduced gamebird, is easier to release and will spread out after a short time; it also performs better than the Grey with bag yields of between 30% and 40% of all released birds. With the Grey Partridge these levels are less common but possibly could be increased using proven techniques and high quality gamekeeping. The Red-Legged Partridge is seen in pockets particularly where rearing for release has occurred; they are less common in Scotland, their main stronghold being in southern England and the arable land of East Anglia. The Chukar Partridge is also an introduced bird, larger than the Red-Legged Partridge and really a specialised bird for a shoot. There is a question mark over the ability of the Chukar and its cross with the Red-Legged to reproduce in the wild. There is little doubt however, that the pure Red-Legged and Grey Partridges will breed in the

101

following year given a fair chance. It is also interesting to note that the Red-Legged Partridge is the only species to double clutch in a season, one for the male, the other for the female to hatch and rear.

Holding Techniques

Christmas is the best time to catch Red-Legs as they tend to disperse more widely, even if they have not been shot regularly; they should be caught up as soon as possible while still in small groups. Having been released from a pen as young stock the adult birds will normally stay near to the food hoppers at the regular feeding stations; these should be closed off and the ground baited round them. Multiple catchers should then be placed alongside the hoppers and also baited with food.

Catching-up Stock Birds

The commonest type of catcher in use is the multiple trap made of Weldmesh or strong plastic netting, secured to a wooden frame 36" x 36" x 18" (1m x 1m x 0.5m) fitted with a tunnel type entrance of a suitable size to just allow the bird to enter. A lid is placed on the top to enable the birds to be removed. All catchers must be inspecteed several times a day, and any birds caught removed and placed in the holding pens. The birds, when caught, should be kept in good condition and overwintered in pens set aside for the purpose. Whichever type of winter penning is used, transfer the selected pairs into the laying pens by the end of February. To obtain the results required it cannot be over stressed that the selection of sound breeding stock is most important; birds out of condition and weak make very poor parents, producing inferior young. Pure-bred Red-Legs can be distinguished from hybrids with the Chukar by the deep necklace of black markings, differences in the flank feathers, and the shade of the back feathers, also the Chukar is larger. The holding pens most gamekeepers seem to use are the moveable type measuring 10' x 6' (3m x 2m) placed on grass.

The Grey Partridge on the other hand does not settle well having been wild caught, and the egg production could well be low, therefore the best method of producing eggs is to retain suitable young stock from the previous year housed in moveable pens at the rate of 10 birds per 10' x 6' pen. With the larger shoots and gamefarms unsexed birds can be kept overwintered in straw yards;

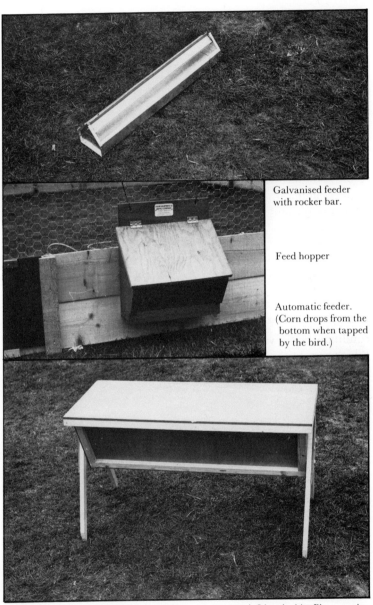

Galvanised feeder
with rocker bar.

Feed hopper

Automatic feeder.
(Corn drops from the
 bottom when tapped
 by the bird.)

Farm Equipment and Supply Company,
Tumby, Boston, Lincolnshire.

c/o Lincolnshire Pheasantries
Mareham-le-Fen (065-83) 218.

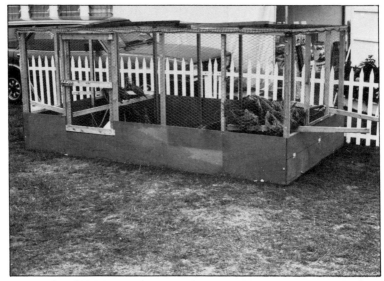

10′ × 5′ Holding or release movable pens suitable for breeding, rearing and release of partridge.

Farm Equipment and Supply Company,
Tumby, Boston, Lincolnshire.

c/o Lincolnshire Pheasantries
Mareham-le-Fen (065-83) 218.

Partridge Pen designed by The Game Conservancy.

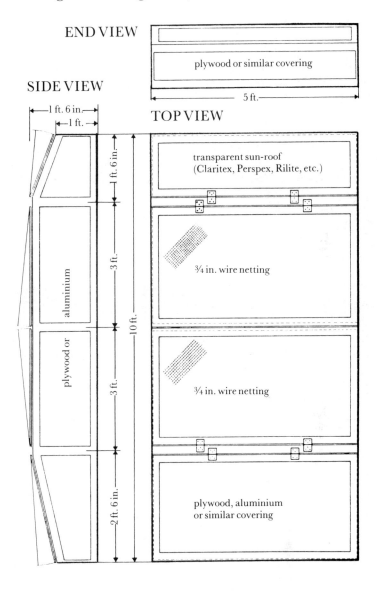

END VIEW

plywood or similar covering

SIDE VIEW

5 ft.

1 ft. 6 in.

1 ft.

TOP VIEW

1 ft. 6 in.

transparent sun-roof
(Claritex, Perspex, Rilite, etc.)

3 ft.

aluminium

10 ft.

¾ in. wire netting

plywood or

3 ft.

¾ in. wire netting

2 ft. 6 in.

plywood, aluminium
or similar covering

this is not recommended as a method to be used on the small estate as disease can become a problem. For guidance the following room is required by each adult bird: The Red-Legged Partridge — 6 - 8 sq.ft., and the Grey Partridge — 10 - 12 sq.ft.

Laying Pens

Red-Legged Partridge can be accommodated in small pens with wire floors measuring 72" long x 16" high x 24" wide (2 x 0.4 x 0.6m). These pens are covered at each end and also include a solid floor compartment, sub-divided into a nestbox and dusting tray. A lid is fitted and hinged at each end, giving access for feeding, watering, and the collection of eggs. The top is covered with ¾" (19mm) mesh plastic netting. Up to six pens can be built side by side in one unit, held off the ground by four legs and can be moved by two men (see diagram Eley laying pens). Hay is placed in the nesting section of the compartment to encourage laying in the area; Red-Legged Partridge usually lay a high proportion of their eggs in the nest area. Remember that the hay must be top quality to reduce the risk of aspergillosis. Unlike the Grey, the Red-Legged Partridge can be flock mated.

The Grey Partridge, on the other hand, needs more room. Some shoots use the overwinter pens divided in two as laying pens, others resort to similar pens to those used for the Red-Legs, but wider in size and lacking the nest compartment, as Greys are disinclined to use one. A sandbox for dusting should be placed under cover in the pen which is quite often used by the birds as a nestbox.

Management: the Laying Pens

To obtain the best results from your stock ad lib feeding and water must be available, together with a supply of insoluble grit. During the first week of March the diet should gradually be changed from Poult Pellets to Breeder Pellets. Most food formulated today includes all the required vitamins, minerals and other essential constituents, therefore before giving any additional grain check with the suppliers, as extra grain could well dilute the additives in the ration. In general the protein level of the food should be between 18% - 19% as a Breeders diet, but where Grey Partridge breeding is practised the correct feed is a pre-requisite. It must be palatable and have a protein level of approx. 20% - 22%. Food intake is important for egg production; should the birds be fed in troughs ensure they are deep enough to prevent them from scratching the food out. If hoppers are used, they should not be so large that the food inside becomes damp and stale before the birds can eat it. Always have plenty of feeders available.

Egg Yields

The first eggs can usually be expected in the last week of March, or the first weeks of April. The average yield from the Grey Partridge is around 36 eggs, whereas the Red-Legged Partridge can exceed 30 eggs per pair, especially with hybrids. The best numbers can be obtained if your stock are housed on wire floors and not grass. Flock-mating of Red-Legs has a lower and less consistent production. Fertility using this method is usually extremely good and the hatch rate satisfactory.

Egg Collection

Eggs should be collected at least three times a day, preferably mid morning, mid afternoon and early evening. This will find most of the eggs. Eggs left on the ground for more than two hours can become contaminated with bacteria on their surfaces, which can cause problems in the incubation; also an egg warmed in the hot sunlight will begin to develop thus upsetting hatchability. Eggs should be washed in an approved egg wash sanitizer, and stored at a temperature of around 55°F. (13°C.). They should be turned once a day, and not stored for more than 10 days, although the first Red-Leg eggs can be left for several weeks until required. To collect eggs from the pens, it is always useful to have a small egg net; this is a small net attached to a stout bamboo cane which can be used to scoop up the egg from the pen without disturbing the birds.

Egg eating

This can occur at any time during the breeding season, and the habit must be stopped otherwise it will spell complete disaster. It is always useful to have at hand a number of china or wooden eggs, which can be placed around the laying pen at the start of the season; this will discourage the would-be egg-eater. There are many ways to stop egg-eating, one used very successfully is the filling of an egg with household mustard and placing it near to where the last one was taken. If the problem persists, an egg filled with dye will show up the culprits which should then be removed as soon as possible.

Disease Control

Breeder pellets do not contain medication to cover Blackhead, Gapes or Coccidiosis, and healthy stock must always be used. However, it is well worth watching for the first signs and treating the birds after consultation with your vet — see chapter 3.

Incubation

Basically there are two ways to hatch your partridge eggs; the first is to use an incubator, which today is run by electricity; the second is to use a bantam. The method you use is really dependent on the number of birds you wish to raise. On some estates, where broodies are sometimes still available, one of the most economic ways of introducing your stock to a shoot is to purchase eggs from a gamefarm, and place them under your own bantams. These should normally be over 90% fertile and hatch well.

The time spent with this operation, however, should not be underestimated, especially when there is normally so much work in hand at that time of the year. For those wishing to raise larger numbers, who do not wish to use bantams, the modern incubator has become quite a reliable piece of equipment, providing it is set up correctly; the general principles are outlined in chapter 6. Incubators are made in various sizes today to accommodate the requirements of most people. The instructions given by the manufacturer must be adhered to if good results are to be obtained.

Hatching

There are basically two types of incubator, a still air type which works on the convection of heated air, and others which have various types of devices to move the air around. The eggs normally would stay in the latter type for 21 days and then be transferred to a hatcher for the last 3 days until the chicks are hatched. The Hatcher is in fact a type of still air incubator, and the machine referred to is usually known as the Setter. For the larger estate and gamefarm the Setter can take many thousands of eggs at a time, the smallest being made takes some 20 - 30 eggs.

The forced air, or Cabinet, incubator (Setter) is normally set up to run at 99.5°F. to 100°F. (37.5° - 37.8°C.), whereas the Still air or Convection type will run at 102°F. - 103.5°F. (39° - 39.5°C.) two inches from the egg tray floor.

It is essential that the amount of moisture in the air of the Setter or Hatcher is correct. Loss of water through the porous shell of the egg during incubation gives the embryo space in which to move just before, and during, hatching. If the air is too damp the air space in the egg will be small, and if too dry, it will be too large, producing a chick which will be sticky and have difficulty in hatching out, conversely a wet egg will virtually drown the embryo. Only when the chicks are dry and fluffy can they be transferred to the brooder. This can be between 12 and 24 hours after hatching. The chicks do not need to feed during that time as they are still living on their egg-sac. However, they should be feeding and drinking properly by 48 hours after hatching, at the latest.

Rearing Chicks

Rearing your chicks using a bantam is well defined, and has been practised by the small shoot owner for many years, so does not need explanation; the basics are covered in chapter 6.

Raising large numbers of Partridge requires warm, dry, clean, draught-proof quarters in which to erect the brooder and a holding circle. Should you not have a suitable out-building in which to house the birds, there are brooder houses made especially for the purpose, which have a covered run for when the chicks are old enough to be allowed outside.

There are a number of types and sizes of brooders available depending on the requirements; for those who do not have electricity, good propane gas heaters are made. The maximum number of chicks one can usually have under one brooder is 500. It is not normal to try and cover so many with one unit — most manufacturers will recommend the number possible. However, should you consider an infra red lamp of 400 watts, it will cover between 70 - 100 chicks. Having decided the way in which the chicks are to be reared, one method which a number of gamefarms use is to erect a circle of hardboard around the brooder, increasing the size of the circle daily until the chicks fly over the sides, at which time the hardboard can be removed. The suggested height for the hardboard is 24" (0.6m). As already mentioned, the source of heat can be an infra-red lamp, but an alternative can be an electric Hen Brooder;

BRISTOL INCUBATORS

Bristol Still Air Incubators and Hatchers have been designed to hatch pheasant, partridge, quail, turkey, fowl and duck eggs. The smaller models can be used as setters and hatchers. The CH.5 has a glass sliding door so that hatching can be observed.

Temperature controls on the CH.5, PH.10 and PH.28 are by low pressure micro switch and one double expanding capsule. There are heating elements above and below the eggs; the heating element under the floor pre-heats the incoming air. Temperature control on the remaining Hatchers is by contact thermometer and electronic relay. These controls have been designed in such a way that, in the event of anything going wrong electrically, there is a back-up safety control if the temperature rises over 99.5°. In such an event all replacement parts are easily plugged in.

Cabinets are made of best quality exterior ply; framework and egg trays are made of best quality hardwood.

The PH.60, PH.90, PH.150 and PH.350 have been designed primarily as still air hatchers only. Normal procedure with these machines is to set eggs in a large forced draught machine and transfer them to the still air hatchers three days prior to hatching. By using this method one can expect a much higher percentage hatch, as the same conditions can be kept in the setter and hatcher throughout the season. It also cuts down on cross-infection. These hatchers are lined with laminate to enable them to be cleaned easily.

All these models are now being used by game farms and game keepers throughout the country and are proving very successful.

Pheasant egg capacities from 600 to 3,500.

Approved by the Game Conservancy

CH.5

Size:	16" x 18" x 11"	
Capacity:	Fowl	45 eggs
	Pheasant	60 eggs
Includes:	1 Egg Tray	
	1 Water Tray	
	1 Double Capsule Temperature Control	

Bristol PH.28 and PH.10 can now be fitted with a fan. This gives the advantage of having a forced draft incubator and still air hatcher in one.

PH.28

Size:	36" x 36" x 17"	
Capacity:	Fowl	170 eggs
	Pheasant	280 eggs
Includes:	2 Egg Trays	
	1 Water Tray	
	2 Surrounds	
	1 Double Capsule Temperature Control	

PH.10

Size:	25" x 25" x 17"	
Capacity:	Fowl	60 eggs
	Pheasant	100 eggs
Includes:	1 Egg Tray	
	1 Water Tray	
	1 Double Capsule Temperature Control	

PATRICK PINKER (Game Farm) LTD.

LATTERIDGE
IRON ACTON
BRISTOL
BS17 1TY   Tel.: RANGEWORTHY 416

this is a square heater element held above the chicks by four adjustable legs, which enables the heat to be reduced as the chicks grow. Some sort of light should be provided to allow the chicks to feed; placing chick crumbs on egg flats provides a certain amount of interest to the chick, but if all else fails, mashed hard boiled egg usually does the trick; try to get them onto standard ration as soon as possible.

The temperature in the centre of the brooder at floor level should be 95°F. (35°C.) with a room temperature of around 75° - 80°F. (24° - 27°C.). The brooder temperature can be reduced by about 5° per week, until the chicks are fully feathered when no heat is required. A simple way to check to see if the temperature is correct, is to observe the chicks and see if they are crowding together, if so, the heat should be increased. Ideally all the chicks should settle in a ring between the hottest point and the outside of the brooder itself.

Food and Water

The standard diet for day-old chicks is a proprietary gamefood or ground turkey starter crumbs of 28% - 29% protein, fed for the first three weeks, but less for Grey Partridge reared indoors. Clean water must be available at all times, this can be achieved by using small glass drinkers. Should there be problems in getting the chicks to feed, try some mashed hard boiled egg mixed with the chick crumbs for the first few days, but do not continue for too long or your birds will prefer egg to crumbs. Another way to stimulate their interest, when dealing with a small number, is to sprinkle some crushed crumbs on their backs as they will then preen and start to eat some of the crumbs. Partridges all prefer to peck at growing vegetation when young, and therefore bantam-raised birds will eat a great deal of white clover from the age of about three weeks, when raised in moveable pens as illustrated. That is not to say, when rearing under intensive conditions, a certain amount of greenery cannot be given.

At the age of three weeks the diet should be changed to a lower protein level and a rearer crumb or pellet of approx. 26% is suitable. When introducing this ration a quantity should be mixed with the old crumbs to help the chicks become accustomed to the new food; start mixing at 2½ weeks.

The 'Lincolnshire' tier system chick and game brooder

Lincolnshire Game Equipment Ltd., Town Road, Tetney, Grimsby, England.   Grimsby (0472) 814472.

ey Partridge with chicks

Painting by Richard Robjent.

ukar Partridge

Red-legged Partridge

Chinese Bamboo Partridge   Painting by Richard Robjent
Male.

See See Partridge   Female.   Altai Snowcock   Paintings By H Grönvol

ELEY Partridge Laying Pen

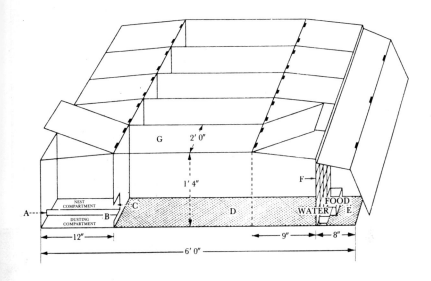

The pens are in batteries of five and should stand on legs to give clearance of at least 9 in. from floor to ground level. A: Strip of batten, 3 in. high. B: Nesting and dusting compartments with solid floor. C: Pophole through partition into nesting area. Measurement is 5 in. square, with a 3 in. sill at the bottom. D: Galvanised wire netting (1 in. mesh). E: Compartment for drinker and feeder, also with wire floor. Lid for this compartment is in one piece for all five pens. F: Screen of ¾ in. mesh Netlon plastic netting (obtainable from garden sundries shops) fastened at bottom to shallow batten. G: Area between lids should be covered with ¾ in. mesh Ulstron netting fastened down with thin wood battens.

Designed by The Game Conservancy
Fordingbridge, Hants.

By the time the chicks have reached one week of age, their food should be placed in metal or similar type containers to prevent wastage. Stale and mouldy food is one of the quickest ways to disaster. In the first few weeks of development some shoots prefer to fit plastic bits to their birds to prevent feather pecking. A 'bit' is a small oval-shaped split plastic ring which clips into the birds' nostrils and at the same time keeps their beaks apart, thus preventing a bird from gripping a feather with its beak, yet still allowing it to feed. (All bits must be removed before release.)

At about six weeks cut wheat may be given in addition to their basic diet, the amount being gradually increased to form half the diet at eight weeks. A further pellet change is now required to reduce the protein level down to 18% - 20%; these are known as grower pellets. Although most food compounds have the required level of calcium grit included it is always worth having a small amount of insoluble grit available to aid the digestion if required. To prepare your stock for release, it is worth starting to feed them from a hopper at about five weeks of age.

Ailments in Young Birds

Salmonellosis

Cause: A specific group of micro-organisms, the salmonellae.

Signs: Bacterium may merely be present causing no signs or losses. May cause an enteritis and heavy losses in chicks. They will huddle under heat, thirsty and weak.

Treatment: Problematical. Consult vet. Antibiotics and drugs may be used. *Note: A notifiable disease.*

'Broken Leg' Syndrome

Cause: So far recorded in Grey Partridge only, *Perdix perdix*. Cause uncertain but too much heat, inactivity in indoor units, too fast growth rate and low Vitamin C are possible.

Signs: Birds suddenly 'go off legs' at about 2½ weeks.

Treatment: Consult vet.

Releasing

The date on which the young birds are taken out to estate to be acclimatised prior to release, will depend on how the corn harvest is progressing. It is advisable to wait until the corn is cut and the straw baled or burned before the Partridge are released, therefore allow at least four weeks between the final release and the first shoot. Grey Partridges can be released when they are eight weeks old, but Red-Legs are better kept up to ten weeks of age before release. Both species should be released after the harvest, except where there are plenty of root fields. This causes some problems in the south of England with a July/August harvest, but the September/October harvest further north is often associated with a more varied cropping pattern, allowing more before-harvest release sites. Grey Partridge seem to be able to tolerate more disturbance than the Red-Legged. Straw burning, particularly during the early morning or evening when the birds are feeding, is a problem to both species.

Method of Release

Where birds have been reared under bantams the usual release method is to use a coop and run. Although giving good results it is a time-consuming method, limited by the supply of good and reliable bantams and suitable equipment. Both species can be released using the 'Caller Bird' technique; transfer the birds to a 10 x 5' moveable pen with shelter at one end. Red-Legs must be hopper fed (thus cutting down disturbance) providing at least one inside and one immediately outside the pen, whereas Greys can be hand fed on a regular basis if required. The same rearing pellets should be used during the main release period, the hoppers being topped up with whole wheat once the birds are at liberty. It is important to provide water drinkers inside and outside all release pens. Red-Legs do better if supplied with a straw bale both inside and outside the pens; this can support the food hopper, but it also allows the birds to 'chatter' to one another.

The principle of the 'caller bird' system is that the original batch of birds is dribbled out through the pophole of the pen over a period of days, leaving two or three birds in the release pen to attract the covey to the pen. The maximum number of Red-Legs should be twenty to be released per pen. During a fine settled spell of weather Red-Legs can be acclimatised for two days after being placed in the pen and then released over the next four or five days at the rate of three per day. In the case of the Grey Partridge a maximum of twelve to fifteen birds can be housed in one pen, allowed to settle for four or five days, and released over a further eight to ten days, at a rate of two per day.

It is generally better to release poults early in the morning, allowing the birds time to get used to their surroundings before the first night. Once released the 'caller birds' can be left in the holding pens until Partridge shooting is over, say in early December.

The cost of stocking a small shoot is likely to fall in real terms as techniques are perfected. Whether it be the purchase of hatching eggs, day old chicks, or seven to nine week old poults, the success of rearing and release will depend on the enthusiasm and ability of the person entrusted with their care.

It is with much appreciation that I thank Keith Chalmers-Watson, of Fenton Barns, North Berwick, East Lothian, Scotland, and the Game Conservancy for their help and advice in writing this chapter.

Note

Should you require additional information on this subject, the Game Conservancy publish the following booklets:-

No 4 Partridge Rearing

No 5 Pheasant and Partridge Eggs: production and incubation.

No 6 Diseases of Gamebirds.

No 18 Red-Legged Partridge.

or contact the Game Conservancy's Field Advisory Service, The Game Conservancy, Fordingbridge, Hants. SP6 1EF. Telephone: Fordingbridge (0425) 52381.

CHAPTER 8

IMPORTATION AND EXPORT OF PARTRIDGE

Before anyone contemplates the importation of Galliformes from any part of the world, they must investigate the current legislation governing the movement of birds from one country to another; the requirements differ between them, as certain parts of the world are considered to have a high disease risk, and to import from these areas can cause problems for the domestic poultry population should disease be brought in. However most governments are helpful, providing importation is not on a large scale and serious breeding is contemplated. In the UK this information can be obtained from the Ministry of Agriculture and Fisheries, Animal Health Division, Government Buildings, Hook Rise, Tolworth, Surrey. They will issue a health certificate for the birds you wish to export, or issue the required licence to import into approved quarantine premises.

Quarantine

When considering the importation of birds, it must be clearly understood that if you offer quarantine facilities up for approval by the Ministry, and they are near your own collection, the Ministry have the right to destroy all of your birds should an imported bird be proven to have died from a notifiable disease. That is of course, assuming your premises have been approved; details of the requirements can be obtained from the above address.

On application the Ministry will send one of their officers to inspect your premises and issue a licence if they are approved. The quarantine period lasts for 35 days starting from the last consignment entering; in certain cases the Ministry may require you to have available a number of young chickens to be used as test birds to be housed with the importation during the 35 days — these will establish whether the imported birds are infected. At the start of and during the quarantine period your local vet will be instructed to visit each week to inspect the birds concerned. Fees are charged by the Ministry for this service.

<table>
<tr><td rowspan="2">SPECIFIC CONTAINER AND HANDLING NOTES</td><td rowspan="2">50</td><td>SECTION:............... IX</td></tr>
<tr><td>PAGE:................. 65
ISSUE DATE:........ JUL 80</td></tr>
</table>

APPLICABLE TO: *(See exception CNG-01 and USG-01 in Section X)*

Francolin
Guinea fowl
Partridge
Pea fowl
Pheasant
Pigeon, large, exotic
Quail, large

Note   For carriage of domestic pets in passenger cabins as accompanied baggage, see Section X — Carrier and Governmental Exceptions.

DESIGN AND CONSTRUCTION

1   **MATERIALS:**

Burlap, hardboard (masonite), plywood and wood.

2   **PRINCIPLES OF DESIGN,** which shall be met in addition to the General Container Requirements in Section VIII:

(a)   Consider the normal habits and necessary freedom of movement in constructing containers for shipment of birds.

(b)   Whenever ventilation holes are to be covered with wire mesh, edges shall have suitable protection to prevent injury to the birds.

(c)   Dimensions where quoted may vary.

(d)   One bird only should be packed in each compartment of the crate, the compartments being of a size to allow the bird to stand upright and to turn round comfortably.

(e)   The floor and front should be made from plywood; the top, sides, partition and back are made from burlap attached to a wooden framework of 3 x 2 centimetres (1.25 x 0.75 inches) wood. If the burlap is closely woven, small holes shall be made in it near the top (e.g. by means of a pencil); if it is of loose weave it will admit sufficient air without the holes. The roof of the crate shall consist of two layers of burlap cloth with some padding (such as fine wood shavings) between them. Alternatively, the sides and top may be made of 3 millimetres (0.125 inch) hardboard or plywood with 2.5 centimetres (1 inch) ventilation holes spaced on all sides, in which case the top must be padded on the inside.

(f)   No doors are necessary. The birds are put in through the unfastened back corners of the roof as illustrated.

(g)   Food and water troughs may be provided. The food and water troughs, if provided, should fit into slots made in the plywood front and shall be attached to the uprights of the framework so that they can be replenished without being removed.

CAUTION: Soldered tin may prove toxic to some birds.

Note   It is recognized that fiberboard containers with ventilation holes are sometimes suitable for game birds, such as pheasant and quail, when shipped on short journeys where watering and feeding is not involved. Accordingly, these fiberboard containers can be used provided that

(i)   The length of time in the container will not exceed 8 hours;

(ii)   No feeding or watering will be required.

118

Endangered Species

There are certain species of Partridge which are on the protected list, and subject to importation under licence. This list is subject to amendment from time to time, and it is therefore worthwhile to apply to the D. of E. for information — The Department of the Environment, Wildlife Conservation Licencing Section, Tolgate House, Houlton Street, Bristol, BS2 9DJ., or your own Fish and Wildlife Services.

Transportation of Birds

There are very strict regulations governing the transport of birds by airlines, and all shipments must comply with I.A.T.A. Regulations. These can be very involved and therefore guidance should be sought from W.P.A. when required. There are some basic requirements which should be noted. The shipper is responsible for seeing that the consignee's full name and address is clearly shown on the Air Waybill; on top of each container he must also attach an I.A.T.A. Live Animals label, correctly completed, and the crate must be clearly marked 'This side up'.

Shipping Documents

Apart from Health Certificates and Licences which together with the Air Waybill are completed by the carrier on behalf of the shipper, you will also be required to complete a Shippers Certification, which details all the basic information on the shipment, i.e. number of crates, description and quantity of birds, name and address of the shipper, origin and destination.

Note: The foregoing must be regarded as for guidance only and not accepted as final. Should an importation be considered seriously you would be well advised to contact the appropriate Ministry for the latest information before embarking on what can be a very expensive project.

CHAPTER 9

THE WORLD PHEASANT ASSOCIATION
QUAIL/PARTRIDGE GROUP

Membership

Membership is open to all those in sympathy with the objectives of the Association who are willing to comply with the rules. W. P. A. is an international organisation designed to enable all interested persons and institutions to participate in fulfilling the objectives of the Association. W. P. A. is fast becoming accepted as the most effective organisation for the conservation of the order of *Galliformes in the world.*

Aims of the Quail/Partridge Group within W. P. A.

1. To bring together those who are interested in the keeping and breeding of captive quail and partridge.
2. To encourage reserve collections and establish a breeding nucleus to ensure a viable breeding pool for the future.
3. To promote sound & improved methods of avicultural husbandry
4. To assist and advise on the management of quail and partridge in captivity.

Advantages of Membership of W. P. A.

These include:-

1. Access to a data bank of information on quail and partridge.
2. Expert advice on all matters pertaining to aviculture of quail/ partridge and related birds.
3. Attending an Annual Convention in Great Britain or elsewhere.
4. The opportunity to visit various collections and conservation areas throughout the world.
5. An annual Journal and three Newsletters a year.
6. The opportunity to participate in special conservation progr- ammes at home and overseas as determined by Council and Governments concerned.
7. Participation at the A. G. M., the election of officers in accordance with the rules of the Association.
8. Other privileges as decided by the Council from time to time.

For subscription details and further information, please write to:- The World Pheasant Association, P.O. Box 5, Church Farm, Lower Basildon, Berkshire RG8 9PF, England. Registered Charity No. 271203. Upper Basildon (049162) 271.

BIBLIOGRAPHY

Salim Ali and S. Dillon Ripley. *Handbook of the Birds of India and Pakistan,* Vol.2. 1980. Oxford University Press, London.

Howard and Moore. *A Complete Checklist of the Birds of the World.* 1980. Oxford University Press, London.

B.E. Smythies. *The Birds of Borneo.* 1981. Oliver and Boyd, Edinburgh, England.

Philip Wildash. *Birds of South Vietnam.* 1968. Charles E. Tuttle Co. Inc., Rutland, Vermont.

Ben F. King and Edward C. Dickinson. *Birds of South-East Asia.* 1975. Houghton Mifflin Co., Boston, U.S.A.

J. Delacour. *Birds of Malaysia.* 1947.

Caldwell and Caldwell. *South China Birds.* 1931.

Clive Roots. *Softbilled Birds.* John Gifford Ltd., London. 1970.

Dr. A.F. Anderson Brown. *The Incubation Book.* Saiga Books, Hindhead, Surrey, England.

W.R. Ogilvie-Grant. *The Handbook to the Gamebirds.* 1896. Edward Lloyd Ltd., Fleet Street, London.

Partridge Rearing. Booklet No. 4.

Pheasant and Partridge Eggs: production and incubation. Booklet No. 5.

Diseases of Gamebirds and Wildlife. Booklet No. 6.

Red-Legged Partridge. Booklet No. 18. The Game Conservancy, Fordingbridge, Hants SP6 1ER.

E.C. Stuart Baker. *The Game Birds of India, Burma, and Ceylon.* The Journal of Bombay, Nat. Hist. Soc. 1920/23.

Ref. 1 ♂ Rock Partridge

Ref. 3 ♂ Przewalski Rock Partridge

Ref. 4 ♂ Philby's Rock Partridge

Ref. 4 ♀ Philby's Rock Partridge

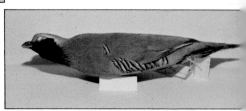

Ref. 5 ♂ Barbary Partridge

Ref. 5 ♀ Barbary Partridge

Ref. 6 ♂ Red-Legged Partridge

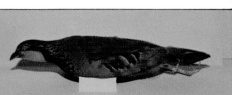

Ref. 7 ♂   Arabian Chukar Partridge

Ref. 8 ♂   See See Partridge

Ref. 8 ♀   See See Partridge

Ref. 9 ♂   Sand Partridge

Ref. 9 ♀   Sand Partridge

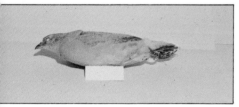

Ref. 11 ♂   Rufous-throated Hill Partridge

Ref. 11 ♀   Rufous-throated Hill Partridge

Ref. 14 ♂   Red-breasted Hill Partridge

Ref. 14 ♀   Red-breasted Hill Partridge

Ref. 15 ♂   Brown-breasted Hill Partridge

Ref. 16 ♂   Boulton's Hill Partridge

Ref. 17 ♂   Ricketts' Hill Partridge

Ref. 17 ♀   Ricketts' Hill Partridge

Ref. 18 ♀   David's Tree Partridge

Ref. 19 ♂   Chestnut-headed Tree Partridge

Ref. 19 ♀   Chestnut-headed Tree Partridge

Ref. 20 ♂   Sumatran Hill Partridge

Ref. 20 ♀   Sumatran Hill Partridge

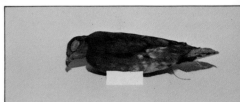

Ref. 21 ♂   Chestnut-bellied Tree Partridge

Ref. 22 ♂   Red-billed Tree Partridge

Ref. 22 ♀   Red-billed Tree Partridge

Ref. 25 ♂   Bamboo Partridge

Ref. 27 ♂   Ferruginous Wood Partridge

Ref. 28 ♂   Crimson-headed Wood Partridge

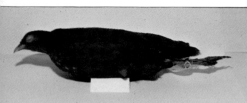

Ref. 28 ♀   Crimson-headed Wood Partridge

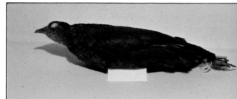

Ref. 29 ♂   Snow Partridge

Ref. 29 ♀   Snow Partridge

Ref. 30 ♂   Madagascar Partridge

Ref. 30 ♀   Madagascar Partridge

Ref. 33 ♂   Daurian Partridge

Ref. 33 ♀   Daurian Partridge

Ref. 34 ♀   Tibetan Partridge

Ref. 35 ♂   Stone Partridge

Ref. 35 ♀   Stone Partridge

Ref. 36 ♂   Long-billed Wood Partridge

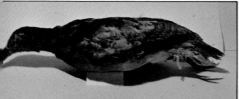

Ref. 36 ♀   Long-billed Wood Partridge

Ref. 38 ♂   Caucasian Snowcock

Ref. 39 ♂   Caspian Snowcock

Ref. 40 ♂   Tibetan Snowcock

Ref. 40 ♀   Tibetan Snowcock

Ref. 41 ♂   Altai Snowcock

Ref. 42 ♂   Himalayan Snowcock

Ref. 42 ♀   Himalayan Snowcock

Ref. 43 ♂   Verreaux's Monal Partridge

Ref. 44 ♂   Széchenyi's Monal Partridge

Ref. 46 ♂   Green-legged Hill Partridge

Ref. 47 ♂   Annamese Hill Partridge